California Family Law Terms

Bakersfield Paralegal & Victor VeVea

Victor VeVea

1706 Chester Ave, Suite 347

Bakersfield, CA 93301

Bakersfield Paralegal – (661) 489-3369

1412 17th St., Ste. 349

Bakersfield, CA 93301

P.O. Box 81

Bakersfield, CA 93302

(661)Justice (587-8423)

A portion of the royalties from this book is used to help victims of domestic violence.

ISBN-13: 978-1-950418-06-0

INTRODUCTION

This book is not meant to be authoritative or comprehensive. It is designed to give definitions, explanations, and examples that are as short and simple as reasonably possible to help readers understand legal terms that are commonly used in family law proceedings.

It is meant for use in the courtroom when you might not be able to access your cell phone but want to quickly learn the meaning of a term.

You should consult with your own attorney for legal advice or to clarify any given term.

ABANDONMENT - CHILD
Definition: In family law, abandonment generally means a parent's intentional failure to provide care, support, or contact under facts that satisfy a particular statute. The required conduct and time period differ among dependency, adoption, guardianship, and proceedings to free a child from parental custody and control.
Explanation: A court may treat a parent's prolonged and intentional absence, lack of support, or lack of communication as abandonment when the requirements of the governing statute are met.
Example: In a stepparent adoption proceeding, the court considered whether the absent parent had left the child in the other parent's care without communication or support for the statutory period.

ABATE
Definition: To reduce, lessen, or diminish the effect of something; in family law, often used to describe the reduction or suspension of spousal support, child support, or legal proceedings due to a change in circumstances.
Explanation: When changed circumstances lead the court to reduce or suspend a payment or legal action.
Example: The court ordered child support to abate while the child was living full time with the other parent.

ABDUCTION BY PARENT
Definition: The unlawful taking, concealment, or retention of a child by one parent in violation of custody rights of the other parent or contrary to a court order.
Explanation: When one parent illegally takes or hides the child from the other parent.
Example: The mother was charged with abduction by parent after taking the child out of state without consent.

ABDUCTION - CHILD
Definition: The wrongful removal or retention of a child from their lawful custodian, including across state or international borders.
Explanation: Taking or keeping a child away from the legal caregiver without permission.
Example: Mother alleged child abduction after Father kept the child overseas.

ABOVE NAMED

Definition: A legal reference to a person, party, or entity already identified earlier in the document, typically used in pleadings, orders, or contracts to avoid repeating the full name.
Explanation: A way of saying "the person already mentioned earlier in the papers."
Example: The court ordered the above named respondent to appear at the custody hearing.

ABUSE - CHILD

Definition: Physical, emotional, or sexual harm to a child, or neglect that threatens the child's health or welfare.
Explanation: Hurting a child or failing to care for the child in a way that is dangerous.
Example: The report alleged child abuse and neglect by the caregiver.
See also: CHILD NEGLECT; CHILD PROTECTIVE SERVICES (CPS); DEPENDENCY.

ABUSE – DOMESTIC VIOLENCE

Definition: Under California's Domestic Violence Prevention Act, abuse includes intentionally or recklessly causing or attempting to cause bodily injury, sexual assault, placing a protected person in reasonable apprehension of imminent serious bodily injury, and conduct that may be enjoined under Family Code §6320, including harassment, stalking, disturbing the peace, and coercive control.
Explanation: Domestic violence may include physical violence, threats, harassment, stalking, coercive control, or other conduct that destroys another person's mental or emotional calm.
Example: She asked for a restraining order due to domestic violence.

ABUSE OF DISCRETION

Definition: A legal standard of review where a higher court finds that a trial judge's decision was arbitrary, unreasonable, or exceeded the bounds of sound judgment, especially when no reasonable judge would have reached the same conclusion.
Explanation: When a judge makes a ruling that is unfair, unreasonable, or clearly outside normal legal judgment.
Example: On appeal, the mother argued that the trial court's denial of her request to relocate was an abuse of discretion because the judge ignored the best interests of the child.

ACCESS
Definition: In some jurisdictions, "access" means visitation or parenting time with a child. California statutes generally use the terms custody, visitation, and parenting time, and any contact order remains subject to the child's health, safety, welfare, and best interests.
Explanation: The term usually describes time or contact with a child, but California courts ordinarily describe that contact as visitation or parenting time.
Example: The divorce decree granted the father access to the child every other weekend and one evening during the week.

ACCOMMODATION
Definition: An adjustment or modification made to ensure fairness or compliance with law; in family law, it often refers to reasonable changes made to meet the needs of a parent, child, or party with a disability so they can fully participate in proceedings or exercise parenting rights.
Explanation: A change or adjustment made so a parent or child can fairly take part in court or parenting, often due to disability or special needs.
Example: The court granted an accommodation allowing the mother, who has a hearing impairment, to use an interpreter during the custody trial.

ACCUSE
Definition: To formally charge or allege that someone has committed a wrongful act; in family law, this may involve claims of child abuse, domestic violence, neglect, or violation of court orders, which must then be proven with evidence.
Explanation: To say that someone has done something wrong or unlawful, such as harming a child or breaking a court order.
Example: During the custody hearing, the father was accused of violating the restraining order by contacting the mother outside of visitation.

ACKNOWLEDGE
Definition: To formally admit, recognize, or declare something as true, valid, or binding; in family law, this often refers to acknowledging parentage, receipt of legal documents, or acceptance of responsibilities imposed by the court.
Explanation: To officially accept or recognize something as true or valid

in court.
Example: The father signed a form to acknowledge paternity of the child, making him legally responsible for support.

ACKNOWLEDGMENT OF PARENTAGE – VOLUNTARY
Definition: A signed legal form by which parents voluntarily establish a legal parent child relationship without a court hearing.
Explanation: A form both parents sign to legally establish parentage.
Example: They signed a voluntary acknowledgment at the hospital to establish parentage.
See also: VOLUNTARY DECLARATION OF PARENTAGE (VDOP); ADJUDICATED PARENT.

ACT OF GOD
Definition: An extraordinary and unforeseeable natural event, such as a flood, earthquake, or storm, that is not caused by human action and cannot be prevented by reasonable foresight or care; in family law, this may affect compliance with court orders, such as visitation or support obligations, when performance is made impossible.
Explanation: A natural event beyond human control, like a disaster, that can prevent someone from following a court order.
Example: The mother explained that she missed the scheduled visitation due to a hurricane, claiming it was an act of God beyond her control.

ACTIVE EFFORTS - ICWA
Definition: The higher level of help that a child welfare agency must provide before an Indian child may be removed from a parent or before parental rights may be ended. The efforts must be active, thorough, timely, and suited to the family's needs and culture.
Explanation: The agency must do more than hand the parent a list of services. It must help the family use services that may keep the child safely at home or return the child home.
Example: The court found active efforts because the social worker arranged tribal services, transportation, treatment, and regular family visits.
See also: INDIAN CHILD WELFARE ACT (ICWA).

ADD ON SUPPORT - CHILD
Definition: Court ordered additional child support for specific expenses such as child care, unreimbursed medical costs, or educational needs.

Explanation: Extra child support to cover things like daycare or medical bills.
Example: The judge ordered child care as an add on support expense.
See also: CHILD SUPPORT; CHILD SUPPORT ADD ONS; MANDATORY AND DISCRETIONARY SUPPORT ADD ONS.

ADDENDUM
Definition: A supplemental document attached to a contract, court order, or agreement that adds to, clarifies, or modifies the original terms without replacing the entire document; in family law, often used in parenting plans, settlement agreements, or support orders.
Explanation: An extra section or addition to legal papers that changes or explains something in the original document.
Example: The parties signed an addendum to their parenting agreement specifying holiday visitation schedules.

ADDRESS
Definition: In legal usage, the location where a party may be served with court papers or contacted for official purposes; in family law, it may also refer to the child's residence for jurisdictional purposes or a parent's disclosure of current residence as required by court orders.
Explanation: The official place where someone can receive legal documents or where a child is considered to live for custody matters.
Example: The custody order required both parents to keep the court informed of their current address to ensure proper notice of hearings.

ADDRESS CONFIDENTIALITY PROGRAM
Definition: A state program that provides a substitute legal address to protect survivors of abuse or stalking.
Explanation: A service that hides a survivor's home address with a safe mailing address.
Example: She enrolled in the address confidentiality program to keep her location private.
See also: CONFIDENTIAL INFORMATION; HOME ADDRESS.

ADDRESS THE COURT
Definition: To speak directly to the judge in a legal proceeding, either orally or in writing, usually for the purpose of making arguments, presenting motions, or responding to questions; in family law, parties, attorneys, and sometimes self represented litigants must properly address

the court when requesting relief or explaining their positions.
Explanation: To formally speak to the judge during a case, asking for something or explaining your side.
Example: During the custody hearing, the mother's attorney asked permission to address the court about the child's medical needs.

ADJOURN
Definition: To suspend or postpone a court proceeding, hearing, or trial to a later time or date, either by order of the judge or by agreement of the parties, usually for good cause such as allowing time for evidence, settlement discussions, or scheduling conflicts.
Explanation: When the judge stops a hearing and moves it to another day or time.
Example: The custody trial was adjourned until the following month to give the evaluator time to complete the home study.

ADJOURNMENT
Definition: The formal act of suspending or postponing a court session, hearing, or trial until a later specified time or date; in family law, adjournments may be granted to allow additional time for mediation, evidence gathering, or the availability of witnesses.
Explanation: The official pause or delay of a court case until another date.
Example: The judge granted an adjournment of the divorce hearing so the parents could attend mediation.
See also: CONTINUANCE.

ADJUDICATE
Definition: To hear and decide a case or issue in a formal legal proceeding, rendering a binding judgment or order; in family law, judges adjudicate matters such as custody disputes, child support, visitation rights, domestic violence restraining orders, and parentage.
Explanation: For a judge to officially decide a legal issue and make it binding.
Example: The family court adjudicated the father's petition for joint custody after reviewing all the evidence.

ADJUDICATED PARENT
Definition: A person whom the court has legally determined to be the child's parent, typically through a parentage action or after genetic testing,

giving that person all legal rights and responsibilities of parenthood.
Explanation: Someone whom the judge has officially declared to be the child's legal parent is called the adjudicated parent.
Example: After reviewing the DNA results, the court named the man the adjudicated parent and ordered him to pay child support.
See also: ACKNOWLEDGMENT OF PARENTAGE – VOLUNTARY.

ADJUDICATION
Definition: The formal judgment or decision of a court resolving a legal matter; in family law, adjudication may determine issues such as child custody, visitation, support obligations, domestic violence findings, or the termination of parental rights.
Explanation: The judge's official decision that settles a family law issue.
Example: The adjudication established the mother as the custodial parent and ordered child support from the father.

ADJUSTMENT
Definition: A modification or change ordered by the court or agreed upon by the parties to reflect new circumstances; in family law, adjustments often apply to child support, spousal support, or parenting time schedules when conditions affecting the family change.
Explanation: A change made to payments or schedules because of new situations in the family.
Example: The court ordered an adjustment to child support after the father lost his job and the mother's income increased.

ADMINISTER AN OATH
Definition: The formal act by which a judge, clerk, or other authorized officer requires a witness, party, or interpreter to swear or affirm that the testimony or statements they provide will be truthful; in family law, this occurs before giving evidence in hearings on custody, support, or domestic violence.
Explanation: When the judge or clerk has someone promise to tell the truth before speaking in court.
Example: Before the social worker testified about the child's living conditions, the clerk administered the oath.

ADMINISTRATIVE OFFICE OF THE COURTS
Definition: "Administrative Office of the Courts" is the former name

commonly used for the staff agency supporting the Judicial Council of California. The Judicial Council is the statewide policymaking body for California's courts, and its staff supports court administration, rules, forms, education, language access, and other branch programs. Local Family Court Services programs are operated through the superior courts.
Explanation: The current statewide administrative body is the Judicial Council of California, supported by Judicial Council staff.
Example: Judicial Council staff developed statewide family law forms and proposed rules for consideration by the Judicial Council.

ADMISSIBILITY
Definition: The legal standard determining whether evidence may be considered by the court, based on rules of relevance, reliability, and conformity with statutes or procedural rules; in family law, admissibility governs whether items such as school records, medical reports, or witness testimony can be used in custody or support hearings.
Explanation: Whether the judge is allowed to accept and consider certain evidence in a case.
Example: The court ruled on the admissibility of the child's therapy records during the custody dispute.
See also: ADMISSIBLE EVIDENCE; INADMISSIBLE; EVIDENCE.

ADMISSIBLE EVIDENCE
Definition: Evidence that meets legal requirements of relevance, reliability, and compliance with evidentiary rules, allowing it to be introduced and considered by the court; in family law, admissible evidence may include financial records, witness testimony, school reports, or expert evaluations directly related to custody, support, or visitation issues.
Explanation: Evidence the judge is legally allowed to accept and use in making a decision.
Example: The judge admitted the parenting coordinator's report as admissible evidence in the custody trial.
See also: ADMISSIBILITY.

ADMONISH
Definition: A formal warning or caution given by a judge to a party, witness, or attorney about their conduct, responsibilities, or rights during legal proceedings; in family law, admonishments may remind parents not

to discuss the case with children or warn litigants to follow court orders.
Explanation: When the judge officially warns someone in court about rules or behavior.
Example: The judge admonished both parents not to make negative comments about each other in front of the child.

ADOPT
Definition: In family law, the legal process by which an adult becomes the lawful parent of a child who is not biologically theirs, creating permanent parental rights and responsibilities and terminating the rights of the biological parents unless otherwise provided by statute.
Explanation: When a court makes someone the legal parent of a child who is not their biological child.
Example: The stepfather petitioned the court to adopt his wife's child, and the judge granted the adoption.

ADOPTION
Definition: A judicial process that permanently establishes a legal parent child relationship between the adoptee and the adoptive parent(s), conferring all parental rights and responsibilities while usually terminating the rights of the biological parents; governed by statutes requiring consents, investigations, and a final decree.
Explanation: When the court makes new parents the child's legal parents forever, giving them all rights and duties.
Example: The family court finalized the adoption of the child after reviewing the home study and consents.
See also: ADOPTION PETITION; ADOPTION FINALIZATION; ADOPTION HOME STUDY; AGENCY ADOPTION; RELINQUISHMENT OF PARENTAL RIGHTS.

ADOPTION ASSISTANCE PROGRAM (AAP)
Definition: A state program that provides financial support to families who adopt children with special needs.
Explanation: Money and benefits to help adoptive families.
Example: The parents received monthly payments under the Adoption Assistance Program.

ADOPTION FINALIZATION
Definition: The court's formal approval and entry of a final decree of adoption, which completes the adoption process, grants the adoptive

parents full legal parental rights and responsibilities, and authorizes the issuance of a new birth certificate for the child.
Explanation: The judge's official order that makes the adoption complete and permanent.
Example: At the hearing, the judge signed the order of adoption finalization, giving the parents full legal rights to the child.
See also: ADOPTION.

ADOPTION PETITION
Definition: A formal written request filed with a court to begin an adoption proceeding and obtain a final adoption order.
Explanation: Paperwork to ask the court to approve an adoption.
Example: They filed an adoption petition to adopt their foster child.
See also: ADOPTION.

ADOPTION SUBSIDY
Definition: Financial assistance provided to eligible adoptive parents to help meet an adopted child's ongoing care, medical, or special needs.
Explanation: Money to help pay for the costs of raising an adopted child.
Example: The family applied for an adoption subsidy to cover medical costs.

ADULT ADOPTION
Definition: An adoption where the person being adopted is over the age of majority, often to formalize an existing parent child relationship.
Explanation: Adopting someone who is already an adult.
Example: The court approved the adult adoption of the caregiver's former foster youth.

ADULT DISABLED CHILD SUPPORT
Definition: Support that both parents may owe for an adult child who cannot earn a living because of a physical or mental disability and who lacks enough other resources. In California, the duty can continue after the usual end of child support.
Explanation: A parent may still have to help support a disabled adult child who cannot support themselves.
Example: The court ordered both parents to share support for their 22 year old child, who could not work because of a severe disability.
See also: AGE OF MAJORITY; CHILD SUPPORT.

ADVOCACY
Definition: The act of representing, supporting, or arguing for the legal rights and interests of a party in court or related proceedings; in family law, advocacy involves presenting evidence, making arguments, and protecting the welfare of children or parents in matters such as custody, visitation, support, or protection orders.
Explanation: Speaking or acting in court on behalf of someone.
Example: The attorney's advocacy focused on demonstrating that joint custody would serve the child's best interests.

AFFIDAVIT
Definition: A written statement of facts made under oath or affirmation and offered as evidence in a legal proceeding.
Explanation: A sworn written statement for the judge to consider.
Example: She filed an affidavit describing the child's medical needs.
See also: DECLARATION; SWORN STATEMENT.

AFFIDAVIT OF SERVICE (PROOF OF SERVICE)
Definition: A sworn written statement confirming when, where, how, and upon whom legal papers were properly served.
Explanation: A signed statement that the other side was served correctly.
Example: She filed an affidavit of service after serving the petition.
See also: PROOF OF SERVICE (AFFIDAVIT OF SERVICE).

AFFIRMATION
Definition: A formal declaration that a statement is true, made by a person who declines to take an oath for religious or personal reasons; in family law, affirmations are often used by witnesses, parties, or professionals submitting reports or testifying in court.
Explanation: A solemn promise to tell the truth without using a religious oath.
Example: The custody evaluator gave an affirmation before testifying about the child's living arrangements.

AFOREMENTIONED
Definition: A legal drafting term used to refer back to a person, party, or matter already identified earlier in the same document, such as a petition, order, or contract, to avoid repetition of full names or details.
Explanation: A way of saying "the person or thing already mentioned

earlier in the document."
Example: The decree stated that the aforementioned minor child would reside primarily with the mother.

AFORESAID
Definition: A formal legal term used in pleadings, contracts, and court orders to refer to a person, party, fact, or matter that has already been mentioned earlier in the same document.
Explanation: Another way of saying "the person or thing already stated above in this document."
Example: The order required the aforesaid respondent to pay child support according to the schedule set by the court.

AGE OF MAJORITY
Definition: The age at which a person is generally treated as a legal adult. In California, the age of majority is 18, but some parental duties and court orders may continue beyond that age, including specified child support obligations for a child still in high school or an adult child who is incapacitated from earning a living and lacks sufficient means.
Explanation: Turning 18 usually creates legal adulthood, but it does not end every family law obligation in every case.
Example: Although the child turned 18, support continued while the unmarried child remained a full time high school student and was not self supporting, subject to the statutory age limit.

AGENCY ADOPTION
Definition: An adoption arranged and supervised through a licensed public or private adoption agency under applicable legal procedures.
Explanation: The process of adopting a child through an agency.
Example: They completed an agency adoption through the county social services department.
See also: INDEPENDENT ADOPTION AGENCY; ADOPTION.

AGREE
Definition: To express mutual consent or acceptance of terms between parties, either orally or in writing; in family law, agreements often cover custody, visitation, child support, spousal support, or property division, and may be incorporated into a court order or judgment.
Explanation: When two or more people accept the same plan or terms, often in writing for the court.

Example: The parents agreed to a shared custody arrangement, and the court entered their agreement as an order.

AGREED JUDGMENT (STIPULATED JUDGMENT)

Definition: A court order reflecting an agreement between the parties that resolves some or all issues.
Explanation: Both sides agree and the judge signs it as a court order.
Example: The parties submitted a stipulated judgment for custody and support.
See also: MARITAL SETTLEMENT AGREEMENT (MSA).

AGREED PARENTING PLAN

Definition: A written agreement between parents outlining custody, visitation schedules, and decision making authority regarding their child, usually approved by the court.
Explanation: A written plan parents make about custody and visitation, approved by a judge.
Example: The court approved the agreed parenting plan that gave both parents equal visitation rights.
See also: PARENTING PLAN.

AGREEMENT

Definition: A mutual understanding or contract between two or more parties, either oral or written, that creates enforceable obligations; in family law, agreements often address custody, visitation schedules, child support, spousal support, or division of community property, and may be incorporated into a final judgment.
Explanation: A deal or understanding between people that sets out what each side must do, often written and approved by the court.
Example: The divorcing spouses signed a settlement agreement dividing property and setting child support, which the court approved.

ALIMONY (SPOUSAL SUPPORT)

Definition: Money one spouse may be ordered to pay the other for support during or after separation or divorce.
Explanation: Payments to help support a spouse.
Example: The court ordered temporary spousal support during the case.
See also: SPOUSAL SUPPORT.

ALLEGATION
Definition: A statement of fact or claim made by a party in a pleading, petition, or motion, which has not yet been proven and must be supported by evidence; in family law, allegations often involve claims of abuse, neglect, domestic violence, or failure to support.
Explanation: Something a person says in court papers that still needs to be proven with evidence.
Example: The mother's petition for custody included an allegation that the father had exposed the child to domestic violence.

ALLEGATIONS OF ABUSE
Definition: Claims made in a family law case that a parent, guardian, or household member has physically, emotionally, or sexually harmed a child or partner.
Explanation: A statement saying someone in the family has abused another person.
Example: The father denied the allegations of abuse raised during the custody hearing.

ALLEGE
Definition: To formally assert or claim something as fact in a pleading, motion, or testimony, subject to proof at trial; in family law, parties may allege issues such as abuse, neglect, interference with visitation, or failure to provide support.
Explanation: To officially state in court papers or testimony that something happened, even though it still must be proven.
Example: In her divorce petition, the wife alleged that the husband failed to pay child support for several months.

ALLEGED PARENT
Definition: A person who is claimed to be a child's parent but whose legal parentage has not yet been established.
Explanation: Someone said to be a parent before the law decides.
Example: Genetic testing was ordered for the alleged parent.

ALLOCUTION
Definition: A formal statement made personally by a party directly to the judge before the imposition of sanctions; in family law, allocution may occur in contempt proceedings, such as when a parent has violated custody or support orders, allowing them to explain or plead for leniency.

Explanation: When a person speaks directly to the judge before being punished, to explain themselves or ask for a lighter outcome.
Example: After being found in contempt for failing to pay child support, the father was given the chance for allocution before the judge imposed sanctions.

ALSO KNOWN AS (AKA)
Definition: A legal designation used to indicate alternative names, aliases, or variations of a person's identity in court documents, ensuring clarity and preventing confusion in records; in family law, it may appear in petitions, orders, or judgments when a party or child is known by more than one name.
Explanation: A way of showing that someone is known by another name in legal papers.
Example: The custody order listed the mother as "Maria Lopez, also known as Maria Torres (AKA)," to match the child's school records.

ALTERNATIVE CUSTODY ARRANGEMENT
Definition: A nontraditional custody plan ordered by the court, such as split custody, bird's nest custody, or rotating schedules, designed to meet the child's best interests.
Explanation: A different type of custody plan instead of the usual sole or joint custody.
Example: The judge approved an alternative custody arrangement where the child stayed in one home while the parents rotated in and out.

ALTERNATIVE DISPUTE RESOLUTION (ADR)
Definition: Methods for resolving legal disputes without trial, including mediation, arbitration, collaborative practice, and judicial settlement conferences.
Explanation: Solving the case without a full trial, often by mediation.
Example: The parties resolved parenting time through mediation as ADR.
See also: MEDIATION; ARBITRATION.

AMEND
Definition: To formally change, revise, or add to a legal document, such as a pleading, petition, motion, or court order, usually with the court's permission; in family law, amendments are often made to custody petitions, support requests, or divorce pleadings to reflect new facts or

relief sought.
Explanation: To officially change or update a legal document filed in court.
Example: The mother filed a motion to amend her custody petition to include new allegations of neglect.

AMENDED PETITION
Definition: A revised pleading that changes or adds to the claims or facts in the original petition.
Explanation: An updated version of the first court filing.
Example: She filed an amended petition to add a request for relocation.

ANNULMENT
Definition: A judicial determination that a marriage was legally invalid or voidable, resulting in a judgment of nullity.
Explanation: A judgment of nullity declares that the marriage was void or voidable under the law; it does not erase the historical fact that a ceremony or relationship occurred.
Example: She sought an annulment based on fraud.

ANSWER
Definition: In general civil litigation, an answer is a pleading that admits, denies, or otherwise responds to allegations in a complaint. In many California family law proceedings, the responding party instead files a Judicial Council "Response," although an "Answer" is used in some proceedings, including certain local child support agency cases.
Explanation: It is the responding party's formal written reply, but the required title and form depend on the type of case.
Example: In the dissolution case, the respondent filed a Response stating which requests were disputed.

ANTI LUCAS STATUTES - SECTIONS 2581 AND 2640
Definition: Current California laws that govern jointly titled property and reimbursement of separate property contributions. Section 2581 usually presumes jointly titled property acquired during marriage is community property, while Section 2640 may reimburse traceable separate property contributions unless reimbursement was waived in writing.
Explanation: Joint title can make property community property, but a spouse may still recover certain separate funds used to buy or improve it.

Example: The home was divided as community property, but Wife received a Section 2640 reimbursement for her documented down payment from an inheritance.
See also: COMMUNITY PROPERTY PRESUMPTION - SECTION 760; VALLI TITLE RULE; TRANSMUTATION / MACDONALD EXPRESS DECLARATION RULE.

APPEAL
Definition: A legal proceeding asking a higher court to review and correct claimed errors in a lower court's decision.
Explanation: Asking another court to look at the judge's decision and fix errors.
Example: She filed an appeal after the custody order was entered.
See also: NOTICE OF APPEAL; APPELLATE REVIEW; STANDARD OF REVIEW.

APPEALS COURT
Definition: "Appeals court" is an informal term for a court that reviews appealable decisions of a lower court. In California, family law appeals from the superior court ordinarily proceed to a California Court of Appeal, not to the superior court's appellate division.
Explanation: In California family law, the reviewing court is usually called the Court of Appeal.
Example: The Court of Appeal reversed the custody order after finding prejudicial legal error.

APPEARANCE
Definition: A party's formal participation in a case, often by filing a notice or attending a hearing.
Explanation: Letting the court know you are part of the case.
Example: Counsel filed a notice of appearance for the respondent.

APPELLANT
Definition: The party who files an appeal, asking a higher court to review and change the decision of a lower court; in family law, an appellant may challenge rulings on custody, visitation, support, property division, or protective orders.
Explanation: The person who lost or disagrees with a lower court's decision and asks a higher court to review it.
Example: The father, as appellant, argued that the trial court abused its

discretion by denying him joint custody.

APPELLATE COURT
Definition: A court with the authority to review the decisions of lower courts to determine whether the law was applied correctly; in family law, Appellate Courts examine issues such as custody determinations, child support calculations, spousal support awards, or property division to ensure fairness and compliance with statutes.
Explanation: A higher court that reviews lower court decisions to check for legal mistakes.
Example: The appellate court affirmed the trial court's order granting the mother sole legal custody.

APPELLATE DIVISION
Definition: In California, the appellate division is a panel of the superior court that reviews limited civil, misdemeanor, and infraction matters. It does not ordinarily decide appeals from family law judgments or orders, which generally go to the Court of Appeal.
Explanation: The superior court's appellate division handles specified lower level civil and criminal appeals, not ordinary family law appeals.
Example: The appellate division reviewed a limited civil judgment, while the family law appeal was filed in the Court of Appeal.

APPELLATE REVIEW
Definition: The process by which a higher court examines the decision of a lower court to determine whether legal or procedural errors occurred that affected the outcome; in family law, appellate review may address rulings on custody, visitation, child support, spousal support, property division, or protective orders.
Explanation: When a higher court looks at a lower court's decision to check if the law was applied correctly.
Example: The appellate review concluded that the trial court erred by failing to consider evidence of domestic violence in the custody decision.
See also: APPEAL.

APPLICANT
Definition: A person who formally submits a request or petition to a court or authority seeking relief, benefits, or an order; in family law, an applicant may seek custody, visitation, child support, spousal support, adoption, or a protective order.

Explanation: The person who files papers in court asking for a legal decision or help.
Example: The applicant filed a petition for a restraining order to protect herself and her children from domestic violence.

APPLICATION
Definition: A formal written request submitted to a court or authority asking for a specific order or relief; in family law, an application may seek custody, visitation, child support, spousal support, adoption approval, or modification of an existing order.
Explanation: A paper filed in court asking the judge to decide or grant something.
Example: The mother filed an application to modify child support after losing her job.

APPOINT
Definition: To designate or assign a person to a particular role or duty by authority of the court; in family law, the court may appoint a guardian ad litem, custody evaluator, mediator, or attorney to represent the child's or a party's best interests.
Explanation: When the judge officially chooses someone to take a legal role in a case.
Example: The court decided to appoint Minor's Counsel to represent the child's best interests in the custody dispute.

APPROVAL
Definition: The formal acceptance or authorization of a request, agreement, or action by a court or authority; in family law, approval is often required for adoption petitions, settlement agreements, parenting plans, or relocation requests.
Explanation: When the court officially agrees to or allows something.
Example: The judge gave approval for the parents' mediated parenting plan to become a court order.

ARBITRATION
Definition: A private dispute resolution process in which a neutral arbitrator hears the parties and issues a binding or nonbinding decision.
Explanation: A neutral person listens and decides the case outside court.
Example: They agreed to arbitration for dividing property.
See also: ALTERNATIVE DISPUTE RESOLUTION (ADR).

ARGUE
Definition: To present reasons, evidence, and legal authority in support of a party's position before the court; in family law, attorneys or self represented parties argue issues such as custody, visitation schedules, support amounts, or protective orders.
Explanation: To explain to the judge why your side is correct, using facts and law.
Example: The mother's attorney argued that granting sole custody to her was in the child's best interests due to the father's history of domestic violence.

ARGUMENTATIVE OBJECTION
Definition: An objection that a question is really an argument, accusation, or comment instead of a fair request for facts. The objection is often made when a lawyer is debating with a witness or asking the witness to accept the lawyer's conclusion.
Explanation: The question is arguing with the witness instead of asking for useful testimony.
Example: Counsel asked, "You did not care whether the children were frightened, did you?" The other attorney objected that the question was argumentative.

ARREARAGE (ARREARS)
Definition: Child support or spousal support payments that became due under an order but remain unpaid.
Explanation: Support money that is late or unpaid.
Example: The order required monthly payments toward the father's child support arrearage from the prior year.
See also: INTEREST ON SUPPORT ARREARS; GARNISHMENT; MONEY JUDGMENT; JACKSON/TRAINOTTI CREDITS.

ASKED AND ANSWERED
Definition: An objection made when a witness has already answered the same question and the question is repeated without a proper reason. The judge may allow repetition when needed to clarify an unclear answer.
Explanation: The lawyer keeps asking a question that the witness already answered.
Example: After Father answered the question twice, the judge sustained an asked and answered objection.

ASSESSMENT
Definition: An evaluation conducted to provide the court with information relevant to a case; in family law, assessments may include custody, psychological, risk, or financial assessments to determine support obligations or the best interests of the child.
Explanation: A professional evaluation that helps the judge decide important issues in a family law case.
Example: The court ordered a psychological assessment of both parents to determine their ability to meet the child's needs.

ASSET DIVISION
Definition: The identification, characterization, valuation, and distribution of community and separate property between spouses during dissolution.
Explanation: Splitting what the couple owns when they divorce.
Example: Asset division included the house equity and retirement accounts.

ASSETS
Definition: All property, tangible or intangible, owned by a person and subject to disclosure and division in family law proceedings; assets may include real estate, bank accounts, retirement funds, vehicles, and personal property, and are characterized as marital, community, or separate depending on jurisdiction.
Explanation: Things of value that a person owns, which the court may divide in divorce.
Example: The court required both spouses to disclose all assets, including retirement accounts and the family home, before dividing property.

ASSIGNED COUNSEL
Definition: An attorney appointed by the court when a constitution, statute, or rule provides a right to counsel. California does not generally appoint free counsel in an ordinary divorce or custody dispute solely because a party cannot afford an attorney, although appointment may be available in proceedings such as juvenile dependency, certain parental rights matters, or contempt proceedings involving a realistic risk of incarceration.
Explanation: Court appointed counsel is available only in specified proceedings; a fee waiver does not itself provide a free lawyer.

Example: The juvenile court appointed counsel for a parent in a dependency proceeding as required by the governing law.

ASSIGNMENT JUDGE
Definition: A judge with administrative authority to assign cases to other judges within a court or division; in family law, the assignment judge may control the calendar and ensure proper distribution of cases like custody or support matters.
Explanation: The judge responsible for deciding which cases go to which courtroom.
Example: The assignment judge directed that all contested custody cases be scheduled for hearing within 90 days.

ASSIGNMENT OF SUPPORT RIGHTS
Definition: The transfer of a person's legal right to collect child support or spousal support to a governmental agency, usually as a condition of receiving public assistance; the agency then seeks reimbursement from the obligated parent.
Explanation: When someone gives the government the right to collect support payments on their behalf.
Example: By accepting public assistance, the mother executed an assignment of support rights to the state agency.

ASSIGNMENT ORDER (EARNINGS ASSIGNMENT)
Definition: A court order directing an employer to withhold support payments directly from an employee's wages and send them to the other parent or state disbursement unit; a common enforcement tool in child and spousal support cases.
Explanation: An order telling an employer to take support money out of a paycheck and send it where it is owed.
Example: The judge issued an assignment order requiring the father's employer to deduct child support from his wages each month.
See also: INCOME WITHHOLDING ORDER.

ASSISTED REPRODUCTION
Definition: Medical methods such as IVF or insemination used to help conceive a child, often with legal agreements.
Explanation: Medical help like IVF to have a baby, with legal rules.
Example: They signed an assisted reproduction agreement before the IVF cycle.

See also: DONOR NOT A PARENT.

ASSUME
Definition: To take on an obligation, duty, or responsibility, either voluntarily or by order of the court; in family law, this may include assuming custody, financial support, or legal responsibilities for a child or spouse.
Explanation: To accept or take on a duty or responsibility in a case.
Example: The stepfather agreed to assume financial responsibility for the child as part of the adoption process.

ASSUMES FACTS NOT IN EVIDENCE
Definition: An objection that a question treats an unproved fact as true. The question may be allowed after evidence supports the assumed fact or if the witness has personal knowledge of it.
Explanation: The question is built on a fact that has not yet been proven.
Example: Counsel asked Mother why she ignored the doctor's warning, but no evidence showed that any warning had been given.

ASSUMPTION
Definition: The act of taking over an existing obligation, responsibility, or role; in family law, assumption may refer to a party taking over child support, spousal support, or caregiving duties by agreement or court order.
Explanation: When someone takes on a duty or role that was previously another's.
Example: The mother sought a court order for the father's assumption of medical expenses for their child.

ATRO (Automatic Temporary Restraining Orders)
Definition: Automatic temporary restraining orders stated in the family law summons under Family Code §2040. They generally restrain specified acts involving removal of minor children, transfer or concealment of property, changes to insurance, and certain nonprobate transfers. They take effect against the petitioner upon filing and against the respondent upon service or other legally sufficient notice.
Explanation: These automatic rules preserve children, property, and insurance while a dissolution, legal separation, or nullity case is pending.
Example: After service of the summons, the respondent could not

remove the children from California without the other parent's written consent or a court order.

ATTACHED
Definition: A legal term indicating that a document, exhibit, or schedule is physically or electronically included with a pleading, petition, or court filing; in family law, attachments often include financial statements, parenting plans, or supporting evidence.
Explanation: Something added to court papers, like a document or schedule.
Example: The parenting plan was attached to the divorce petition for the judge's review.

ATTEST
Definition: To formally declare or certify that a document, signature, or statement is genuine, accurate, or true, usually by signing as a witness or official; in family law, clerks and notaries often attest to affidavits, agreements, or sworn statements.
Explanation: To officially confirm that something is true or properly signed.
Example: The clerk attested to the mother's signature on the voluntary parentage acknowledgment.

ATTORNEY
Definition: A person licensed by the state to practice law and represent clients in legal proceedings; in family law, attorneys advise and advocate for parties in matters such as divorce, custody, child support, spousal support, adoption, and protective orders.
Explanation: A lawyer who represents and advises someone in a family law case.
Example: The mother hired an attorney to represent her in the custody dispute.

ATTORNEY CLIENT PRIVILEGE
Definition: A legal doctrine that protects confidential communications between an attorney and their client made for the purpose of obtaining or giving legal advice; in family law, this privilege prevents disclosure of private discussions about custody, divorce strategy, or settlement negotiations.
Explanation: A rule that keeps what a client tells their lawyer private and

protected from disclosure.
Example: The mother's discussions with her attorney about settlement strategy were protected by attorney client privilege.
See also: ATTORNEY WORK PRODUCT; PRIVILEGE LOG.

ATTORNEY OF RECORD
Definition: The lawyer officially designated in court filings as representing a party in a case; the attorney of record receives all legal notices, is responsible for pleadings, and appears formally in the proceedings.
Explanation: The lawyer officially listed in court documents as the representative for a party.
Example: All motions were served on the father's attorney of record, as required by court rules.

ATTORNEY'S FEES AND COSTS
Definition: The compensation paid for legal services and related expenses incurred in litigation, which may be ordered by the court to be paid by one party to another; in family law, fees and costs may be awarded based on financial need, ability to pay, bad faith conduct, or statutory provisions.
Explanation: The money a party must pay for lawyer services and court expenses, sometimes ordered to be covered by the other side.
Example: The judge ordered the father to pay a portion of the mother's attorney's fees and costs due to his higher income.
See also: COSTS AND ATTORNEY FEES; BORSON MOTION; FAMILY LAW ATTORNEY'S REAL PROPERTY LIEN (FLARPL).

ATTORNEY WORK PRODUCT
Definition: Legal protection for an attorney's writings, research, notes, impressions, conclusions, opinions, and case strategy prepared for a client or lawsuit. Some work product is absolutely protected, while other material may be discoverable only on a strong showing of need and unfair hardship.
Explanation: The other side usually cannot obtain a lawyer's private case strategy or mental impressions.
Example: The court denied a demand for counsel's interview notes because they contained protected attorney work product.
See also: ATTORNEY CLIENT PRIVILEGE.

AUTHORITY

Definition: The legal right or power granted by law, rule, or court to make decisions or take actions; in family law, authority may refer to parental authority over a child, judicial authority to issue orders, or statutory authority for enforcement.
Explanation: The legal power to make decisions or act in a case.
Example: The court held that it had authority to decide custody because the child had lived in the state for six months.

AUTHORIZATION

Definition: Official permission or approval to take a specific action; in family law, authorization may include consent for medical treatment, permission to travel with a child, or court approved access to records.
Explanation: Permission granted by a court or party to do something legally.
Example: The judge required written authorization before either parent could take the child out of the country.

AWARD

Definition: The decision of a court or arbitrator granting relief, rights, or money; in family law, awards may include custody, visitation, child support, spousal support, attorney's fees, or division of property.
Explanation: What the judge gives to one party in a case, such as money or custody rights.
Example: The court made an award of primary physical custody to the mother and child support to be paid by the father.

BATTERER INTERVENTION PROGRAM (BIP)

Definition: A court ordered educational and counseling program designed for individuals who have committed acts of domestic violence, focusing on accountability, behavior change, and prevention of future abuse; in family law, completion of a BIP may be required as part of custody or visitation orders.
Explanation: A program of classes and counseling ordered by the court for people who committed domestic violence.
Example: The father was required to complete a Batterer Intervention Program before unsupervised visitation could resume.
See also: DOMESTIC VIOLENCE; SUPERVISED VISITATION.

BEHAVIORAL HEALTH EVALUATION
Definition: A professional assessment conducted by a psychologist, psychiatrist, or licensed clinician to evaluate a party's mental health, substance use, or behavioral functioning; in family law, courts order such evaluations when concerns about parenting ability, safety, or stability arise.
Explanation: A mental health check by a professional to help the court decide if a parent can safely care for a child.
Example: The court ordered a behavioral health evaluation of the mother due to concerns about substance abuse.

BENCH
Definition: The judge's seat in a courtroom, often used as a metonym for the judicial authority itself; in family law, "the bench" refers to the judge presiding over cases such as divorce, custody, support, or domestic violence.
Explanation: The place where the judge sits in court, also meaning the judge's authority.
Example: The bench emphasized that the child's best interests are the primary concern in custody disputes.

BENCH CONFERENCE
Definition: A private discussion at the judge's bench between the judge and attorneys, often outside the hearing of the parties or public; in family law, bench conferences may cover sensitive issues such as evidentiary objections or settlement discussions.
Explanation: A private talk between the judge and lawyers, usually not heard by others in the courtroom.
Example: The judge called a bench conference to discuss whether certain testimony about the child was admissible.

BENCH TRIAL
Definition: A trial in which the judge, rather than a jury, serves as the factfinder, hearing the evidence and rendering a decision; in family law, most cases such as divorce, custody, and support are bench trials.
Explanation: A trial decided only by the judge without a jury.
Example: The custody dispute proceeded as a bench trial, and the judge decided which parent should have primary custody.

BENCH WARRANT
Definition: A warrant issued by a judge authorizing arrest after a person fails to appear or obey a court directive.
Explanation: An order to arrest someone who missed court.
Example: A bench warrant issued after he failed to appear for the hearing.

BENEFICIARY
Definition: A person who is entitled to benefits or assets under a legal arrangement such as a trust or insurance policy.
Explanation: The person who receives money or property from a trust or policy.
Example: The child was named as the beneficiary of the life insurance.

BEST EVIDENCE RULE
Definition: A rule concerning proof of the content of a writing, recording, or photograph. California generally requires the original when its content is being proved, but duplicates and other secondary evidence may be admissible under statutory exceptions.
Explanation: The original is generally preferred to prove what a document says, but the evidence rules allow copies or other proof in many circumstances.
Example: A duplicate of the custody order was admitted after no genuine question was raised about its authenticity and no rule required the original.

BEST INTEREST FACTORS
Definition: The statutory criteria a court considers to decide what custody and visitation arrangement serves the child's best interests.
Explanation: The list of things the judge looks at to protect the child's well being.
Example: The judge reviewed best interest factors before setting the schedule.
See also: BEST INTERESTS OF THE CHILD.

BEST INTERESTS HEARING
Definition: A court proceeding to determine what custody or visitation arrangement best serves the child's needs and welfare.
Explanation: A hearing to decide what is best for the child.
Example: At the best interests hearing, the judge focused on the child's

schooling and health needs.
See also: BEST INTERESTS OF THE CHILD.

BEST INTERESTS OF THE CHILD
Definition: The guiding standard that custody and visitation orders must prioritize the child's health, safety, and welfare.
Explanation: Courts put the child's needs first when making orders.
Example: The order was based on the child's best interests because the child needed speech therapy.
See also: BEST INTEREST FACTORS; BEST INTERESTS HEARING; FREQUENT AND CONTINUING CONTACT.

BEYOND THE SCOPE
Definition: An objection that a question goes outside the subjects covered by the prior examination or outside the proper limits of the hearing. A judge may still allow the question if it concerns a relevant issue and orderly procedure permits it.
Explanation: The question goes farther than the earlier testimony or the issue the court is hearing.
Example: On redirect, counsel began asking about bank accounts that had not been discussed on cross examination, and the other side objected that the questions were beyond the scope.

BIFURCATION
Definition: Separating one issue (like marital status) from the other issues in a case so it can be decided sooner.
Explanation: Splitting part of the case to decide it earlier.
Example: The court granted bifurcation of marital status before property division.

BIOLOGICAL PARENT
Definition: A person genetically related to a child, although biological connection alone does not always establish legal parentage.
Explanation: The parent by birth or genetics.
Example: The biological parent consented to the adoption.

BIRTH CERTIFICATE
Definition: An official vital record of a child's birth. It may list parents, but the appearance of a name on a birth certificate does not necessarily establish or conclusively determine legal parentage; parentage may require

a valid Voluntary Declaration of Parentage or a court order.
Explanation: A birth certificate records birth information, but legal parentage may have to be established separately.
Example: The father's name was added to the birth certificate after paternity was established.

BIRTH CERTIFICATE AMENDMENT
Definition: A legal change to the information on a birth certificate, such as parentage or name, based on a court order or vital records process.
Explanation: Updating a birth record after a court order or legal process.
Example: After adoption, they filed for a birth certificate amendment.

BIRTH PARENT
Definition: The person who gave birth to the child or the genetic parent, depending on the legal context.
Explanation: The child's parent by birth.
Example: The birth parent signed a consent to adoption.

BOND (GUARDIAN'S BOND)
Definition: A surety bond posted by a guardian of the estate to protect the child's property from loss or misuse.
Explanation: Insurance like protection for money managed by a guardian.
Example: The guardian posted a bond before accessing the child's funds.

BONDING STUDY
Definition: A professional evaluation of the emotional attachment and relationship between a child and a parent or caregiver.
Explanation: A study to see how close a child feels to a parent or caregiver.
Example: The court ordered a bonding study to evaluate attachment.

BORSON MOTION
Definition: A request based on In re Marriage of Borson for a Family Court fee award payable directly to a former attorney for services already provided. The request is limited and generally requires that the former attorney still be counsel of record and act with the client's express or implied approval.

Explanation: A former family law attorney may sometimes ask the court to order payment of earned fees directly to the attorney.
Example: Before being formally substituted out, counsel filed a Borson motion with the client's approval for unpaid fees already earned in the case.
See also: ATTORNEY'S FEES AND COSTS.

BRANCO CREDITS
Definition: "Branco credits" is informal shorthand sometimes used for the community property interest recognized in In re Marriage of Branco (1996) 47 Cal.App.4th 1621. Branco applied the Moore/Marsden approach when community credit and funds were used to refinance and pay an obligation secured by one spouse's separate real property, giving the community a proportionate interest rather than a simple postseparation reimbursement for maintaining community property.
Explanation: When community resources reduce debt on separate real property, the community may acquire a proportionate reimbursement and appreciation interest under Moore/Marsden principles.
Example: Community funds used to refinance and reduce the mortgage on a spouse's separate residence created a community interest calculated under Moore/Marsden principles.
See also: MOORE/MARSDEN; EPSTEIN CREDITS.

BRIEF (LEGAL)
Definition: A written legal argument presenting relevant facts, governing law, analysis, and requested relief to a court.
Explanation: A paper lawyers write to explain their side to the judge.
Example: The attorney filed a brief in the custody dispute.

BROWN TIME RULE
Definition: A method associated with In re Marriage of Brown for dividing pension benefits earned partly during marriage. The community share is often based on the employee's service during marriage compared with total service, although the proper formula depends on the retirement plan and the benefit involved.
Explanation: The court often divides a pension by comparing married service time with the employee's total service time.
Example: Because 12 of the employee's 24 years of credited service occurred during marriage, the court used a time rule to calculate the community share.

See also: DEFINED BENEFIT PLAN.

BROWN & YANA THRESHOLD SHOWING

Definition: A rule from In re Marriage of Brown & Yana that may require a parent opposing a move to first show possible detriment to the child or a material change of circumstances before receiving a full custody trial. It usually applies when a final order gives the moving parent sole physical custody.
Explanation: The parent opposing a move may need to show real possible harm before the court holds a full move away trial.
Example: Father did not receive a full evidentiary hearing because he offered no facts showing that Mother's proposed move would harm the child.

BURDEN OF PROOF

Definition: The level of evidence a party must present to persuade the court, such as preponderance of the evidence or clear and convincing evidence.
Explanation: How much proof you need to win an issue.
Example: The moving party did not meet the burden of proof for modification.

BURGESS RULE

Definition: A move away rule from In re Marriage of Burgess. A parent seeking to relocate with a child does not have to prove that the move is necessary. In a proper postjudgment case involving sole physical custody, the custodial parent may move unless the move would prejudice the child's rights or welfare.
Explanation: A custodial parent usually does not have to prove the move is required, but the child's welfare still controls.
Example: The court did not demand proof that Mother's job transfer was necessary, but it still examined how the move would affect the child.
See also: MOVE AWAY CASE.

BUSINESS RECORDS EXCEPTION

Definition: An exception to the hearsay rule that allows admission of regularly kept business records, such as medical or school records.
Explanation: A rule that lets the judge accept records like school or medical files without live testimony.
Example: The school records were admitted under the business records

exception.
See also: HEARSAY.

BUSINESS VALUATION
Definition: An expert appraisal of a business's value for property division or support calculations in divorce.
Explanation: Figuring out what a business is worth for divorce purposes.
Example: The court considered expert business valuation in dividing assets.
See also: PEREIRA METHOD; PROFESSIONAL GOODWILL.

BUYOUT (MARITAL HOME BUYOUT)
Definition: One spouse pays the other for their share of community equity to keep an asset like the marital home.
Explanation: Paying a spouse for their share so one person keeps the house.
Example: They arranged a buyout of the marital residence.
See also: EQUALIZATION PAYMENT.

CALENDAR
Definition: The official schedule of cases, hearings, or trials set by the court for specific dates; in family law, the calendar organizes divorce trials, custody hearings, child support conferences, and domestic violence proceedings.
Explanation: The court's schedule that shows when cases will be heard.
Example: The judge set the custody hearing on the family court calendar for next month.

CALLS FOR SPECULATION
Definition: An objection that a question asks a witness to guess about facts, motives, future events, or another person's thoughts without a reliable basis. A witness may testify to reasonable opinions only when the evidence rules allow it.
Explanation: The witness is being asked to guess instead of testify from knowledge or a proper opinion.
Example: The judge sustained the objection when a neighbor was asked what Father intended to do next year.

CAPACITY TO CONSENT
Definition: The legal ability of a person to understand, appreciate, and voluntarily agree to an act, order, or contract; in family law, this may arise in issues such as marriage validity, consent to adoption, or medical treatment for a child.
Explanation: The ability of a person to understand and agree to something in a way the law recognizes.
Example: The court examined whether the teenager had the capacity to consent to her own medical treatment.

CAPTION
Definition: The heading of a legal document that identifies the court, case number, and names of the parties; in family law, captions appear on petitions, motions, and orders in cases such as divorce, custody, or adoption.
Explanation: The heading at the top of court papers that shows the court, case number, and parties.
Example: The caption of the divorce petition listed both spouses as parties to the case.

CARNEY RULE
Definition: A custody rule from In re Marriage of Carney that forbids courts from treating a parent's physical disability as automatic proof of unfitness. The court must examine the parent's actual abilities, available help, and the disability's real effect on the child's care.
Explanation: A disability alone does not make a parent unfit. The court must look at how the parent actually cares for the child.
Example: The judge considered Father's adaptive equipment and support network instead of assuming his wheelchair use prevented safe parenting.

CASA (COURT APPOINTED SPECIAL ADVOCATE)
Definition: A trained volunteer appointed by the court to advocate for the best interests of children in cases of abuse, neglect, or dependency; CASAs investigate, report to the court, and make recommendations on custody and placement.
Explanation: A volunteer chosen by the court to speak up for a child's best interests in difficult cases.
Example: The CASA recommended that the child remain in foster care until reunification could safely occur.

CASE
Definition: A legal dispute brought before a court for resolution; in family law, a case may involve divorce, custody, child support, spousal support, adoption, guardianship, or protective orders.
Explanation: A legal matter filed in court to be decided by a judge.
Example: The divorce case included issues of custody, support, and property division.

CASE LAW
Definition: The body of prior judicial decisions that establish legal principles and precedents applied in later cases; in family law, case law guides judges on issues such as custody standards, relocation, child support calculations, and equitable distribution.
Explanation: Past court decisions that judges use to decide similar new cases.
Example: The judge relied on case law holding that the best interests of the child are the primary custody standard.

CASE MANAGEMENT CONFERENCE (CMC)
Definition: A court hearing used to review case status, address deadlines, manage discovery, and promote efficient resolution.
Explanation: A short hearing where the judge checks progress and plans next steps.
Example: At the CMC, the court set discovery and mediation dates.

CASE MANAGEMENT ORDER (FAMILY COURT)
Definition: An order from the Family Court that sets deadlines and procedures for how a case will proceed, including hearings and required filings.
Explanation: An order describing how a family case will proceed.
Example: The judge issued a case management order scheduling mediation and discovery deadlines.

CASE PLAN
Definition: A written child welfare plan identifying services, visitation arrangements, safety objectives, and permanency goals for the family.
Explanation: A plan the court uses in child protection cases to guide services and visits.
Example: The social worker submitted the case plan for court approval.

CASE WORKER
Definition: A social services professional assigned to investigate, monitor, and support families in cases involving child welfare, abuse, neglect, or foster care; in family law, case workers provide reports and recommendations to the court.
Explanation: A professional who helps and monitors families in child related court cases.
Example: The case worker recommended supervised visitation after investigating allegations of neglect.

CASELOAD
Definition: The total number of cases assigned to a judge, attorney, or case worker at a given time; in family law, heavy caseloads can delay hearings and evaluations.
Explanation: The number of cases a judge, lawyer, or case worker is handling.
Example: Due to a heavy caseload, the family court postponed the custody hearing.

CEASE AND DESIST
Definition: A demand that a person stop specified conduct. It may be an attorney or party letter, an agency directive, or part of a court order; the phrase itself does not automatically mean that a judge has issued an enforceable order.
Explanation: It is a formal demand to stop conduct, but enforceability depends on who issued it and the legal authority behind it.
Example: Counsel sent a cease and desist letter demanding that the repeated harassing messages stop and warning that protective relief would be requested.

CERTIFICATION
Definition: An official document or statement confirming that a fact, record, or copy is true and accurate; in family law, certifications are often used for birth records, income statements, or compliance with court orders.
Explanation: An official confirmation that something is true or correct.
Example: The attorney submitted a certification of the mother's income to support the child support claim.

CERTIFIED COPY
Definition: A reproduction of a document that has been officially verified as a true and exact copy of the original; in family law, certified copies are required for documents like marriage certificates, divorce decrees, or adoption orders.
Explanation: An official copy of a document confirmed to be the same as the original.
Example: The adoptive parents submitted a certified copy of the child's birth certificate to the court.

CERTIORARI
Definition: A discretionary writ by which the United States Supreme Court may review a decision of a federal court of appeals or a state court of last resort. California state appellate review ordinarily proceeds by appeal or by a petition for an extraordinary writ, not by a petition for certiorari to a California court.
Explanation: A party asks the United States Supreme Court to choose whether to review a qualifying lower court decision.
Example: After the state supreme court proceedings ended, the parent petitioned the United States Supreme Court for a writ of certiorari on a federal constitutional issue.

CHAIN OF CUSTODY
Definition: The documented process that records the handling, transfer, and storage of evidence from collection to presentation in court, ensuring its authenticity; in family law, this can apply to drug tests, medical records, or supervised visitation logs.
Explanation: A record showing who handled evidence and when, to prove it is reliable.
Example: The mother's attorney questioned the chain of custody for the father's drug test results.
See also: EVIDENCE CODE SECTION 403 OBJECTION.

CHALLENGE
Definition: A legal objection or contest to evidence, testimony, or a judicial decision; in family law, challenges may be raised to custody evaluations, admissibility of records, or a judge's impartiality.
Explanation: To formally object to something in a case.
Example: The father's attorney filed a challenge to the custody evaluator's report, arguing bias.

CHAMBERS
Definition: The private office or courtroom space of a judge where certain discussions, conferences, or proceedings may take place outside of open court; in family law, chambers conferences often handle settlement talks or sensitive matters.
Explanation: The judge's private office where some case discussions happen.
Example: The parties met in chambers with the judge to discuss settlement of visitation issues.

CHANGE OF CIRCUMSTANCES
Definition: A significant change in facts or conditions that may justify modifying a custody or support order.
Explanation: A big change in life that could cause the judge to change orders.
Example: The father got custody based on a change of circumstances.
See also: CUSTODY MODIFICATION; MOTION TO MODIFY SUPPORT.

CHANGE OF VENUE
Definition: The legal process of transferring a case from one court or jurisdiction to another, usually because of concerns about fairness, convenience, or proper jurisdiction; in family law, a change of venue may be requested if the child now resides in a different county or state, or if all parties have moved.
Explanation: When a case is moved from one court location to another for fairness or convenience.
Example: The mother requested a change of venue for the custody case after both parents relocated to another county.

CHILD ABDUCTION PREVENTION ORDER
Definition: Court orders designed to reduce the risk that a parent will wrongfully remove or hide a child.
Explanation: Rules to prevent a parent from taking or hiding the child.
Example: The order required surrender of the child's passport as prevention.

CHILD CUSTODY
Definition: The allocation of legal custody (the authority to make decisions concerning a child's health, education, and welfare) and physical

custody (where and with whom the child lives). Family Code sections 3003 through 3007 define these forms of custody; section 3100 separately governs reasonable visitation.
Explanation: Legal custody concerns major decisions; physical custody concerns the child's residence and day to day care.
Example: They share joint legal custody but have different physical schedules.
See also: CUSTODY; LEGAL CUSTODY; PARENTING TIME.

CHILD CUSTODY EVALUATION
Definition: A professional assessment of a family's circumstances and parenting capacities to assist the court in deciding custody and parenting time.
Explanation: A professional studies the family and makes recommendations to the judge.
Example: The evaluator interviewed both parents and the child.

CHILD CUSTODY MEDIATION REPORT
Definition: A written report prepared by a mediator summarizing parents' discussions and recommendations about custody and visitation.
Explanation: The mediator's written summary of what was discussed about custody.
Example: The court reviewed the child custody mediation report before making a final decision.

CHILD CUSTODY RECOMMENDING COUNSELING (CCRC)
Definition: Court connected custody counseling required before many contested custody hearings in California. The counselor helps parents seek agreement. In a recommending county, the counselor may give the judge recommendations if no agreement is reached; in a confidential program, the counselor generally does not recommend an outcome.
Explanation: Parents meet with a court counselor before the judge decides custody, and local rules determine whether the counselor may make recommendations.
Example: The parents reached no agreement in CCRC, so the recommending counselor sent a proposed parenting plan to the court.
See also: FAMILY COURT SERVICES; MEDIATION.

CHILD DEVELOPMENT ASSESSMENT
Definition: An evaluation of a child's physical, emotional, social, and educational progress, often ordered in custody or dependency cases.
Explanation: An evaluation to see how a child is growing and developing.
Example: The judge ordered a child development assessment to help decide custody.

CHILD ENDANGERMENT
Definition: Putting a child's health, safety, or welfare at risk through neglect, abuse, or exposing the child to dangerous conditions.
Explanation: When an adult puts a child in danger by neglect or abuse.
Example: He was arrested for child endangerment after leaving his toddler alone in the car.
See also: CHILD PROTECTION ORDER; CHILD PROTECTIVE SERVICES (CPS).

CHILD EXCHANGE PROGRAM (NEUTRAL SITE)
Definition: A supervised service or designated safe location where parents exchange their child for visitation to reduce conflict or risk of harm.
Explanation: A safe place where parents switch custody of the child.
Example: The parents used a child exchange program at a neutral site to avoid direct conflict.
See also: MONITORED EXCHANGE.

CHILD MAINTENANCE (ALTERNATE TERM FOR SUPPORT)
Definition: Payments made by one parent to contribute to the child's living expenses and needs; another term for child support.
Explanation: Money a parent pays to help support the child's needs.
Example: The father was ordered to pay child maintenance until the child turned 18.

CHILD NEGLECT
Definition: Failure of a parent or caregiver to provide proper care, supervision, or essential needs of a child.
Explanation: When a parent doesn't give a child food, shelter, or care.
Example: The agency investigated allegations of child neglect.
See also: ABUSE - CHILD.

CHILD PROTECTION ORDER
Definition: A court order that protects a child from abuse, neglect, or exposure to domestic violence by limiting or restricting contact with the alleged abuser.
Explanation: A court order to keep a child safe from harm or abuse.
Example: The court issued a child protection order after evidence of neglect was found.
See also: CHILD ENDANGERMENT.

CHILD PROTECTIVE SERVICES (CPS)
Definition: A governmental agency that receives and investigates reports of suspected child abuse or neglect and takes protective action when legally authorized.
Explanation: The agency that looks into child abuse and keeps children safe.
Example: CPS opened an investigation after the hotline call.
See also: ABUSE - CHILD; CHILD ENDANGERMENT.

CHILD SUPPORT
Definition: Court ordered financial support paid for a child's care and living expenses, generally based on both parents' incomes and parenting arrangements.
Explanation: Money to help pay for a child's needs.
Example: The guideline child support amount was ordered.
See also: ADD ON SUPPORT - CHILD; CHILD SUPPORT GUIDELINES DEVIATION; CHILD SUPPORT GUIDELINE; ADULT DISABLED CHILD SUPPORT; FAMILY SUPPORT.

CHILD SUPPORT ADD ONS
Definition: Additional child related costs such as child care, uninsured medical expenses, or educational costs that parents share.
Explanation: Extra costs for the child that parents split.
Example: They split child care and uninsured medical expenses as add ons.
See also: ADD ON SUPPORT - CHILD; MANDATORY AND DISCRETIONARY SUPPORT ADD ONS.

CHILD SUPPORT FORMULA VARIABLES (K, HN, H%, TN)
Definition: Terms used in California's statewide child support formula. HN is the high earner's net monthly disposable income, H% is that

parent's approximate share of primary physical responsibility, TN is both parents' combined net monthly disposable income, and K is the amount of combined income allocated for support.
Explanation: The support calculator uses both parents' net income and parenting time, along with a legal allocation factor.
Example: The court corrected H% after finding that Father's actual parenting schedule was 35 percent, not the 50 percent entered in the first calculation.
See also: CHILD SUPPORT GUIDELINE.

CHILD SUPPORT GUIDELINE
Definition: A statutory formula used to calculate the presumptively correct amount of child support based on required financial and parenting factors.
Explanation: A legal formula the judge uses to set support.
Example: The court applied the guideline to compute support.
See also: CHILD SUPPORT; CHILD SUPPORT FORMULA VARIABLES (K, HN, H%, TN); NET DISPOSABLE INCOME; CHILD SUPPORT GUIDELINES DEVIATION; LOW INCOME ADJUSTMENT.

CHILD SUPPORT GUIDELINES DEVIATION
Definition: A court approved change from standard child support guidelines due to special circumstances such as medical or educational needs.
Explanation: Changing the normal child support amount because of special needs.
Example: The court allowed a deviation due to the child's high medical expenses.
See also: CHILD SUPPORT; CHILD SUPPORT GUIDELINE; HIGH EARNER EXCEPTION; HARDSHIP DEDUCTION.

CIRCUMSTANTIAL EVIDENCE
Definition: Indirect evidence that does not directly prove a fact but allows a judge to infer its existence from related facts or circumstances; in family law, circumstantial evidence may be used to show neglect, abuse, or unfitness when direct proof is unavailable.
Explanation: Proof that suggests something happened based on related facts, not direct observation.
Example: The judge considered circumstantial evidence of the father's

alcohol use, such as empty bottles found in the home, when ruling on custody.
See also: EVIDENCE.

CITATION
Definition: A written order or notice requiring a person to appear in court, or a reference to legal authority (such as case law or statute) in legal documents; in family law, citations are used both to compel attendance and to support legal arguments.
Explanation: Either a paper telling someone to go to court, or a reference to laws or cases in legal documents.
Example: The father received a citation to appear in court for failing to pay child support.

CITE
Definition: To formally reference or quote a statute, regulation, case law, or other authority to support a legal argument; in family law, attorneys cite statutes or prior decisions to show how the law applies to custody, support, or divorce cases.
Explanation: To point to a law or past case in order to support an argument in court.
Example: The mother's attorney cited case law to argue that relocation should be denied because it was not in the child's best interests.

CIVIL HARASSMENT RESTRAINING ORDER (CHRO)
Definition: A protective order under Code of Civil Procedure §527.6 for unlawful violence, a credible threat of violence, or a knowing and willful course of conduct that seriously alarms, annoys, or harasses and serves no legitimate purpose. It is commonly used when the relationship does not qualify for a domestic violence restraining order, although other specialized protective-order statutes may apply.
Explanation: It can protect a person from qualifying harassment or violence, often involving a neighbor, acquaintance, or more distant relative.
Example: She filed a CHRO against her neighbor for threats.
See also: CYBER HARASSMENT.

CLAIM
Definition: A demand for relief, right, or remedy asserted in court by one party against another; in family law, claims may involve requests for

custody, visitation, child support, spousal support, or division of property.
Explanation: A legal request asking the court to decide or grant something in a case.
Example: The mother filed a claim for increased child support based on the father's higher income.

CLAIMANT
Definition: The person who asserts a claim in court and seeks relief or enforcement of rights; in family law, a claimant may be a parent requesting custody, support, or enforcement of an order.
Explanation: The person who brings a request to the court asking for something.
Example: The claimant asked the court to enforce the custody order after repeated violations.

CLEAR AND CONVINCING EVIDENCE
Definition: A heightened standard of proof requiring evidence strong enough to produce a firm belief or conviction that the fact is highly probable. It is used in specified family and juvenile proceedings, including many proceedings to terminate parental rights, but ordinary domestic violence findings are not categorically governed by this standard.
Explanation: Stronger proof than "more likely than not" but less than "beyond a reasonable doubt."
Example: The judge required clear and convincing evidence before terminating the father's parental rights.

CLERK'S OFFICE
Definition: The administrative office of the court where clerks manage case records, filings, and public access to court documents; in family law, parties go to the clerk's office to file petitions, motions, or obtain certified documents.
Explanation: The office in the courthouse where paperwork is filed and records are kept.
Example: The mother went to the clerk's office to file her motion to modify custody.

CLETS ENTRY
Definition: The process of entering a restraining order into the California Law Enforcement Telecommunications System so police can

enforce it.
Explanation: Putting the restraining order into the police database for enforcement.
Example: The clerk ensured the DVRO was entered into CLETS.
See also: FIREARMS RELINQUISHMENT ORDER.

CLOSING ARGUMENT
Definition: The final statement made by each party's attorney (or by a self represented litigant) at the end of a hearing or trial, summarizing the evidence and explaining how the law supports their position; in family law, closing arguments emphasize factors such as the best interests of the child, financial fairness, or safety concerns.
Explanation: The last chance for lawyers or parties to tell the judge why the decision should be in their favor, based on the evidence.
Example: In her closing argument, the mother's attorney stressed that joint custody was not in the child's best interests due to the father's history of domestic violence.

CO PARENTING AGREEMENT
Definition: A written agreement between separated or divorced parents on how they will share responsibilities for raising their child.
Explanation: Parents' written plan on raising their child together after separation.
Example: Their co parenting agreement included holiday schedules and health care decisions.

COERCIVE CONTROL
Definition: A pattern of conduct that unreasonably interferes with another person's free will and personal liberty. Under California's domestic violence law, it can include isolation, monitoring, threats, financial control, deprivation of basic needs, compelled conduct, or reproductive coercion, even without physical injury.
Explanation: Abuse can be a pattern of control that takes away a person's freedom, not only hitting or threats of physical harm.
Example: The court found coercive control where Husband tracked Wife's location, controlled all money, blocked family contact, and threatened to take the children.
See also: DOMESTIC VIOLENCE; REPRODUCTIVE COERCION.

COHABITATION
Definition: Living together in an intimate relationship without marriage, which may affect support, property, or contractual claims.
Explanation: Unmarried partners living together, which can change support.
Example: The court considered cohabitation when reviewing spousal support.

COHABITATION AGREEMENT
Definition: A written contract between unmarried partners living together that sets out their rights and responsibilities, similar to a marital contract.
Explanation: A contract between unmarried partners about their shared responsibilities.
Example: They signed a cohabitation agreement to clarify financial duties while living together.

COLLABORATIVE DIVORCE
Definition: A divorce process where both spouses and their lawyers work together cooperatively to resolve disputes without trial.
Explanation: A divorce where both sides agree to work together instead of going to trial.
Example: They chose collaborative divorce to avoid a stressful courtroom battle.

COLLABORATIVE LAW
Definition: A process where parties and their lawyers agree to resolve family disputes cooperatively without litigation.
Explanation: Everyone works together with lawyers to settle without going to trial.
Example: They used collaborative law to resolve property and custody issues.

COLLATERAL ATTACK
Definition: A legal challenge to a judgment made in a separate proceeding rather than through a direct appeal; in family law, a collateral attack may occur when a party questions the validity of a custody order, adoption decree, or support judgment in a different case or jurisdiction.
Explanation: Challenging a past court decision in a different case instead of appealing it directly.

Example: The father attempted a collateral attack on the adoption decree by claiming the court lacked jurisdiction years earlier.

COLLATERAL REVIEW
Definition: A judicial examination of the validity of a prior judgment or decision in a new proceeding, often to assess whether the earlier case complied with constitutional or jurisdictional requirements; in family law, this may apply to reviewing older custody or support orders.
Explanation: When a court looks at a past judgment in a new case to check if it was legally valid.
Example: The appellate court conducted a collateral review of the dependency order after claims of due process violations.

COMMINGLING
Definition: The mixing of separate and community property in the same account or asset. Commingling does not automatically convert separate property into community property if the separate contribution can be adequately traced and no valid transmutation occurred; inability to trace may prevent the spouse from proving a separate property claim.
Explanation: Mixing funds can make ownership harder to prove, but good records may preserve a traceable separate property interest.
Example: Although the inheritance was deposited into a joint account, bank records traced the funds to the purchase, so the court recognized the separate property contribution.
See also: SEPARATE PROPERTY; DIRECT TRACING / FAMILY EXPENSE PRESUMPTION; INHERITANCE.

COMMISSIONER AS TEMPORARY JUDGE
Definition: A court commissioner who hears and decides a matter as a temporary judge after the parties consent, either expressly or as allowed by law. A party should understand whether consent is being requested because a temporary judge may enter binding orders like a Superior Court judge.
Explanation: A commissioner may act as the judge when the parties legally consent to that role.
Example: At the start of the hearing, both parties signed a stipulation allowing the commissioner to sit as a temporary judge.

COMMUNITY DEBTS
Definition: Debts assigned to the community estate under California

law. Debts incurred by either spouse before separation are generally divided as community obligations, subject to statutory exceptions, reimbursement rules, and distinctions between allocation of the debt between spouses and a creditor's right to collect.
Explanation: Many debts incurred before separation are divided between the spouses, but exceptions and creditor rights can change the result.
Example: The court divided the couple's credit card balances as community debts in the divorce decree.

COMMUNITY PROPERTY
Definition: Property and earnings acquired by either spouse during marriage while domiciled in California, unless a statutory exception or valid agreement applies.
Explanation: Most things earned or bought during marriage belong to both spouses.
Example: The court divided community property equally.
See also: QUASI-COMMUNITY PROPERTY; SEPARATE PROPERTY; COMMUNITY PROPERTY PRESUMPTION - SECTION 760; DATE OF SEPARATION.

COMMUNITY PROPERTY PRESUMPTION - SECTION 760
Definition: The California rule that property acquired by a married person while domiciled in California during marriage is generally community property unless a statute or valid agreement provides otherwise. The person claiming separate property usually must prove the separate character.
Explanation: Most property earned or bought during a California marriage is presumed to belong to both spouses.
Example: Because the account was funded with wages earned during marriage, the court treated it as community property unless Husband could trace separate funds.
See also: COMMUNITY PROPERTY; ANTI LUCAS STATUTES - SECTIONS 2581 AND 2640.

COMMUNITY PROPERTY WAIVER
Definition: An agreement in which one spouse voluntarily gives up rights to community property, often part of a marital settlement or contract.
Explanation: When one spouse agrees not to claim shared community

property.
Example: She signed a community property waiver as part of her divorce settlement.

COMPETENT EVIDENCE
Definition: Evidence that is legally admissible and sufficient to prove a fact in court, meeting standards of relevance and reliability; in family law, competent evidence includes testimony, documents, or expert reports that the court can consider in custody, support, or divorce cases.
Explanation: Evidence the judge is allowed to use to decide a case.
Example: The custody evaluator's report was admitted as competent evidence in the custody dispute.

COMPETING PARENTAGE PRESUMPTIONS
Definition: A situation in which more than one person qualifies for a legal parentage presumption. The court weighs the competing presumptions based on policy, logic, the child's relationships, and the child's best interests, and in a proper case may recognize more than two parents.
Explanation: When two or more people have strong legal claims to parentage, the judge decides which claim or claims should control for the child.
Example: The court weighed the birth spouse's marital presumption against another person's long standing presumed parent relationship with the child.
See also: PARENTAGE BY HOLDING OUT; THREE PARENT FINDING.

COMPLAINANT
Definition: The person who initiates a legal complaint or petition seeking relief from the court; in family law, a complainant may request divorce, custody, support, or protective orders.
Explanation: The person who files a complaint or petition asking the court for help.
Example: The complainant filed for a restraining order to protect herself and her children from domestic violence.

COMPLIANCE
Definition: The act of following or obeying a court order, rule, or legal requirement; in family law, compliance may involve paying support on time, following visitation schedules, or obeying restraining orders.

Explanation: Doing what the court has ordered.
Example: The father demonstrated compliance by making all child support payments on schedule.

COMPLY
Definition: To act in accordance with or fulfill the requirements of a law, order, or regulation; in family law, a party must comply with custody schedules, support obligations, and protective orders.
Explanation: To follow what the court requires.
Example: The mother was warned to comply with the visitation schedule or face sanctions.

COMPOUND QUESTION
Definition: An objection that one question asks two or more separate things, making a single answer unclear or unfair. The judge may require the questioner to divide it into separate questions.
Explanation: The question combines several questions and should be broken apart.
Example: Counsel asked whether Mother missed the appointment and refused to call the doctor, so the court required two separate questions.

COMPULSORY MEDIATION
Definition: A requirement by the court that parties attempt mediation before proceeding to trial in a family law case.
Explanation: The judge requires mediation before allowing trial to begin.
Example: The court ordered compulsory mediation before scheduling the custody hearing.
See also: MEDIATION.

CONCERNING
Definition: A legal drafting term used to indicate that a statement, order, or document relates to a particular subject or party; in family law, it may appear in decrees or agreements referring to custody, support, or visitation issues.
Explanation: A formal way of saying "about" or "related to" in legal documents.
Example: The order included provisions concerning the child's schooling and medical care.

CONDON SAFEGUARDS
Definition: Protective terms used in some international move away cases under In re Marriage of Condon. They may include consent to California jurisdiction, a bond, passport controls, detailed travel terms, payment of travel costs, and steps to improve recognition and enforcement of the California order abroad.
Explanation: When a child moves to another country, the court may add protections so California orders can still be followed and enforced.
Example: The move away order required Mother to post a bond, preserve the child's United States passport, and submit to California jurisdiction.
See also: RELOCATION.

CONFIDENTIAL INFORMATION
Definition: Sensitive information that is protected from public disclosure, often by statute or court order; in family law, this includes addresses of abuse survivors, financial account numbers, or children's medical records.
Explanation: Private information that must be kept secret and not shared publicly.
Example: The custody file contained confidential information such as the child's therapy records.
See also: ADDRESS CONFIDENTIALITY PROGRAM.

CONFIDENTIAL PERSONAL IDENTIFIER
Definition: A piece of personal data, such as Social Security numbers, driver's license numbers, or financial account numbers, that must be protected in legal filings; in family law, courts require redaction of such identifiers to protect privacy.
Explanation: Personal numbers or details that must be hidden in court papers to protect privacy.
Example: The court ordered parties to redact all confidential personal identifiers from financial records.

CONFLICT OF INTEREST
Definition: A situation where a person's professional or personal interests could improperly influence their judgment or responsibilities; in family law, conflicts of interest may arise with attorneys, guardians ad litem, or evaluators who have ties to one party.
Explanation: When someone involved in a case cannot be fair because

of personal or professional connections.
Example: The attorney withdrew from representing the mother due to a conflict of interest with the father.

CONFORMED COPY
Definition: A copy of a filed document stamped to show it matches the document on file with the court.
Explanation: A stamped copy proving it's the same as the court's version.
Example: She kept a conformed copy of the judgment for records.

CONSENT
Definition: Voluntary agreement or approval by a person with legal capacity to an action, order, or arrangement; in family law, consent may apply to parenting plans, adoption, medical treatment for children, or settlement agreements.
Explanation: When someone agrees to something willingly and legally.
Example: Both parents gave their consent to the child's relocation out of state.

CONSOLIDATED ACTION
Definition: The joining of two or more related legal cases into one proceeding to improve efficiency, avoid conflicting rulings, and reduce costs; in family law, cases involving the same parties, such as divorce and custody, may be consolidated.
Explanation: When the court combines related cases into one case.
Example: The divorce action and the custody petition were merged into a consolidated action.

CONTEMPT OF COURT
Definition: Willful disobedience of a court's order or showing disrespect to the authority of the court; in family law, contempt may arise from failing to pay support, violating visitation schedules, or ignoring restraining orders.
Explanation: When someone knowingly disobeys a judge's order or shows disrespect to the court.
Example: The father was found in contempt of court for refusing to pay child support as ordered.
See also: SANCTIONS FOR DISOBEYING COURT ORDER; WILLFUL CONTEMPT; VIOLATION OF COURT ORDER.

CONTEST
Definition: To formally challenge, oppose, or dispute a legal claim or proceeding; in family law, parties may contest divorce grounds, custody petitions, or support claims.
Explanation: To fight against or disagree with a claim in court.
Example: The mother decided to contest the father's request for sole custody.

CONTESTED DIVORCE
Definition: A divorce where the parties cannot agree on issues such as property, custody, or support.
Explanation: A divorce with disagreements that must be decided by the court.
Example: They went through a contested divorce involving custody disputes.

CONTINUANCE
Definition: A court authorized postponement of a hearing, trial, or deadline to a later date or time.
Explanation: Moving a court date to another day.
Example: The judge granted a continuance to allow time for mediation.
See also: CONTINUE A HEARING; ADJOURNMENT.

CONTINUE A HEARING
Definition: A postponement of a scheduled court hearing to a later date, ordered by the judge for good cause such as lack of evidence, attorney conflicts, or the need for more preparation.
Explanation: When the judge delays a hearing to another day.
Example: The court agreed to continue the custody hearing so the evaluator's report could be completed.
See also: CONTINUANCE.

CONTINUING DUTY OF DISCLOSURE
Definition: The ongoing duty of divorcing spouses to update material information about assets, debts, income, expenses, investment opportunities, and changes that affect the case. The duty continues until each issue is finally resolved, not only when the first disclosure forms are exchanged.
Explanation: A spouse must keep financial information current throughout the case.

Example: Husband had to disclose the new stock award he received before the property settlement was completed.
See also: OMITTED ASSET OR DEBT; FELDMAN DISCLOSURE SANCTIONS.

CONTROLLING SUPPORT ORDER - UIFSA
Definition: The one support order that governs current enforcement when courts in more than one state have issued support orders for the same parties and child. UIFSA provides rules for identifying the controlling order and the amount of unpaid support.
Explanation: When several states have support orders, the court decides which single order controls going forward.
Example: California recognized the Nevada order as controlling and calculated arrears under that order before enforcement.

COSTS AND ATTORNEY FEES
Definition: The expenses of litigation, including court filing fees and payments for legal representation, which the court may order one party to pay to the other in family law cases depending on financial need, ability to pay, or misconduct.
Explanation: The money for lawyer services and court expenses, which one side may have to pay for the other.
Example: The judge ordered the father to pay part of the mother's costs and attorney fees because of his higher income.
See also: ATTORNEY'S FEES AND COSTS.

COUNSEL
Definition: A lawyer or attorney who represents a party in a legal matter; in family law, counsel provides advice, prepares documents, and advocates in court.
Explanation: Another word for lawyer.
Example: The mother's counsel argued that joint custody was not in the child's best interests.

COUNSELING
Definition: Professional therapy or guidance services provided to individuals or families; in family law, courts may order counseling for children, parents, or entire families to address issues like divorce, visitation, or domestic violence.
Explanation: Therapy or advice sessions ordered or recommended by

the court.
Example: The judge ordered family counseling to help the children adjust to the divorce.

COURT
Definition: A tribunal established by law to hear and decide disputes, interpret laws, and issue legally binding orders; in family law, the court resolves matters such as divorce, custody, visitation, adoption, and protective orders.
Explanation: The official place where judges decide legal disputes.
Example: The family court ruled on custody and child support during the divorce.

COURT ADMINISTRATOR
Definition: A court official responsible for overseeing the administration, scheduling, and management of cases and staff to ensure efficient operation of the court system.
Explanation: The person who helps manage the court's schedule and operations.
Example: The court administrator coordinated the family court calendar to reduce delays.

COURT APPEARANCE
Definition: The formal act of attending court at a scheduled time and place, either personally or through legal counsel, to participate in proceedings.
Explanation: When someone shows up in court for their case.
Example: The father failed to make his required court appearance for the support hearing.
See also: APPEARANCE.

COURT APPOINTED EVALUATOR
Definition: A professional such as a psychologist or social worker appointed by the court to evaluate the family situation and make recommendations about custody or visitation.
Explanation: An expert chosen by the court to study the family and suggest custody plans.
Example: The court appointed evaluator recommended joint custody after interviewing both parents and the child.

COURT CLERK
Definition: An officer of the court who manages filings, keeps records, swears in witnesses, and provides administrative support to judges and attorneys.
Explanation: The court official who handles paperwork and records.
Example: The court clerk filed the divorce petition and issued the case number.

COURT COSTS
Definition: Mandatory fees and expenses charged for using the court system, such as filing fees, service fees, and transcript costs; sometimes ordered to be paid by one party.
Explanation: The fees required to file and process a case in court.
Example: The father was ordered to pay the court costs for the divorce action.

COURT DEADLINES
Definition: The time limits established by law or court order within which parties must file documents, respond, or complete actions; missing a deadline may result in dismissal or sanctions.
Explanation: The due dates for filing or responding to court papers.
Example: The mother missed the court deadline to file her response to the custody petition.

COURT INTERPRETER
Definition: A trained and certified professional who translates spoken or signed language in court proceedings to ensure parties and witnesses with limited English proficiency or disabilities can fully participate.
Explanation: A person who translates what is said in court so everyone understands.
Example: The court appointed a court interpreter to assist the mother who spoke only Spanish.

COURT INTERPRETING SERVICES
Definition: Services provided by certified interpreters to assist non English speakers or individuals with hearing impairments during court proceedings, ensuring access to justice.
Explanation: Interpreter services in court for those who do not speak English or have hearing difficulties.
Example: The family court provided court interpreting services for the

father who spoke only Mandarin.

COURT ORDER
Definition: A legally binding directive issued by a judge requiring or prohibiting specific actions; in family law, court orders cover custody, visitation, support, property division, or protective measures.
Explanation: A judge's official command that must be followed.
Example: The father violated the court order by failing to return the child on time.
See also: MINUTE ORDER; FINDINGS AND ORDER AFTER HEARING (FOAH).

COURT ORDERED SUPERVISED VISITATION
Definition: Visitation that must occur in the presence of an approved third party or agency for safety.
Explanation: Visits with the child happen only when a supervisor is present.
Example: Due to safety concerns, visits were supervised at an agency.
See also: SUPERVISED VISITATION.

COURT RECORDS
Definition: The official documents and materials that make up the history of a case, including pleadings, motions, evidence, orders, and judgments.
Explanation: The official file containing all documents from a case.
Example: The adoption court records were sealed to protect the child's privacy.

COURT REPORTER
Definition: A professional responsible for creating a verbatim transcript of court proceedings, ensuring an accurate and official record.
Explanation: A person who types or records everything said in court.
Example: The court reporter prepared a transcript of the custody hearing for the appeal.

COURT RULES
Definition: The procedural rules and regulations governing how cases are filed, heard, and decided in a particular court system; they ensure consistency and fairness in legal proceedings.
Explanation: The rules that explain how court cases must be handled.

Example: The mother's attorney cited court rules requiring timely disclosure of financial records.

COURTHOUSE
Definition: The building where judicial proceedings are held, housing courtrooms, clerk's offices, and administrative offices; in family law, the courthouse is the place where parties file petitions, attend hearings, and participate in trials involving custody, support, divorce, or adoption.
Explanation: The official building where people go for court cases.
Example: The mother went to the courthouse to file her motion to modify custody.

COURTROOM
Definition: The specific room within a courthouse where a judge conducts hearings and trials, takes evidence, and issues rulings; in family law, courtrooms are where disputes over custody, support, visitation, and protective orders are decided.
Explanation: The room where the judge hears cases and makes decisions.
Example: The custody trial took place in the family courtroom before Judge Ramirez.

CROSS EXAMINATION
Definition: The questioning of a witness by the opposing party's attorney after the witness has given direct testimony, intended to test credibility, reveal inconsistencies, or clarify facts; in family law, cross examination is used to challenge testimony about custody, visitation, abuse, or financial issues.
Explanation: When the other side's lawyer asks questions to check if a witness is telling the truth or to point out weaknesses in their story.
Example: During cross examination, the father's attorney questioned the mother's expert about errors in the custody evaluation.
See also: DIRECT EXAMINATION.

CUSTODIAL PARENT
Definition: The parent with whom a child primarily resides or who exercises the greater share of physical custody.
Explanation: The parent the child lives with most of the time.
Example: Mother is the custodial parent during the school year.
See also: NONCUSTODIAL PARENT.

CUSTODY
Definition: The legal and practical responsibility for the care, control, and upbringing of a child, which may include legal custody (decision making authority regarding education, health, and welfare) and physical custody (where and with whom the child lives); custody orders are determined by the court based on the best interests of the child.
Explanation: The legal right and duty to care for and make decisions about a child.
Example: The court awarded joint legal custody but granted the mother primary physical custody of the child.
See also: CHILD CUSTODY; LEGAL DECISION MAKING; PARENTING TIME.

CUSTODY MODIFICATION
Definition: A request or order changing an existing custody or visitation arrangement. After a final judicial custody determination, the requesting parent generally must show a significant change of circumstances affecting the child's best interests; a temporary or clearly nonfinal order may be reconsidered under the best interests standard without the same threshold showing.
Explanation: The required showing depends on whether the existing custody order is truly final or only temporary.
Example: Father requested modification after moving closer to the child's school.
See also: CHANGE OF CIRCUMSTANCES; MONTENEGRO CHANGED CIRCUMSTANCES RULE; MODIFICATION.

CUSTODY SWAP LOCATION
Definition: A designated public or safe place where parents exchange custody of their child to minimize conflict and ensure safety.
Explanation: A set safe place where parents switch custody of the child.
Example: The parents agreed to use a police station as their custody swap location.
See also: MONITORED EXCHANGE.

CYBER HARASSMENT
Definition: The use of electronic communication (such as emails, text messages, or social media) to intimidate, threaten, or harass another person; in family law, cyber harassment may be grounds for protective orders, restrictions on communication, or custody determinations when it

affects a child's welfare.
Explanation: When someone uses the internet or electronic messages to threaten or bother another person.
Example: The court issued a restraining order after finding that the father's repeated threatening emails to the mother constituted cyber harassment.
See also: HARASSMENT; CIVIL HARASSMENT RESTRAINING ORDER (CHRO).

DAMAGES
Definition: Monetary compensation awarded for legally recognized harm. Family courts primarily grant remedies authorized by the Family Code; separate tort damages for assault, domestic violence, emotional distress, or other civil wrongs are ordinarily sought through an appropriate civil claim, subject to joinder, jurisdiction, and procedural rules.
Explanation: Money the court orders one person to pay another for harm or loss caused.
Example: The spouse pursued a related civil claim for medical expenses and other damages arising from an alleged assault.

DATE OF SEPARATION
Definition: The date when a complete and final break in the marital relationship occurred. California looks for one spouse's expressed intent to end the marriage and conduct consistent with that intent. The date can affect whether later earnings, debts, or property are community or separate.
Explanation: It is the date the marriage truly ended in both intent and conduct, even before the divorce became final.
Example: The court found the date of separation was March 1, when Wife clearly ended the marriage and the parties began living separate financial lives.
See also: SEPARATE PROPERTY; COMMUNITY PROPERTY.

DE FACTO PARENT
Definition: A person who has acted as a child's day to day parent and formed a strong parental bond, most often in a juvenile dependency case. De facto parent status may allow participation in hearings and access to some information, but it does not create full legal parentage or an automatic right to custody.

Explanation: A long term caregiver may be allowed to take part in the child's court case without becoming a legal parent.
Example: The juvenile court granted the aunt de facto parent status after she had provided daily care for the child for three years.

DEADLINE
Definition: A fixed time limit set by statute, rule, or court order within which a party must take a required legal action, such as filing documents or paying support; failure to meet a deadline may result in penalties or dismissal.
Explanation: The last day or time by which something must be done in a court case.
Example: The father missed the deadline to file his response to the custody petition.

DEAL
Definition: An informal term for an agreement or settlement reached between parties, often finalized in a written stipulation or consent judgment; in family law, deals may involve custody schedules, support amounts, or property division.
Explanation: An agreement reached between the parties, often later approved by the judge.
Example: The parents made a deal to share summer visitation equally, which was later entered as a court order.

DEBT
Definition: A financial obligation to pay money owed to another person or entity; in family law, debts incurred during marriage may be classified as community/marital debts and divided between spouses, while individual debts may remain separate.
Explanation: Money that a person owes to another person, business, or institution.
Example: The court divided the couple's credit card debt as part of the divorce settlement.

DECLARATION
Definition: A written statement submitted to the court under penalty of perjury, similar to an affidavit.
Explanation: A written statement to the court sworn as true.
Example: She filed a declaration explaining why custody should change.

See also: AFFIDAVIT.

DECLARATORY JUDGMENT
Definition: A binding judgment issued by a court that declares the rights, duties, or obligations of the parties without ordering enforcement or awarding damages; in family law, declaratory judgments may be used to establish marital status, determine the validity of a prenuptial agreement, or clarify parental rights.
Explanation: A court's official statement that explains what the law says about the parties' rights, without giving money or punishment.
Example: The family court entered a declaratory judgment confirming that the prenuptial agreement was valid.

DECREE
Definition: A formal and authoritative order of the court that resolves a case or specific issue; in family law, decrees include divorce decrees, custody decrees, and adoption decrees, which finalize the court's rulings and carry the force of law.
Explanation: A judge's official written order that ends or settles a case.
Example: The judge signed a decree of divorce that included custody and child support provisions.

DECREE OF DIVORCE
Definition: The final judgment entered by a court that legally terminates a marriage and resolves reserved issues.
Explanation: The court's final order that a marriage is over.
Example: The decree of divorce was signed by the judge last month.

DEDUCTION
Definition: A subtraction or reduction from income, wages, or benefits, often for tax or support purposes; in family law, deductions may include amounts withheld from earnings for child support, spousal support, or health insurance premiums.
Explanation: Money taken out of income or pay for support, taxes, or other required purposes.
Example: The court ordered a deduction from the father's paycheck each month for child support.

DEED
Definition: A written and signed legal document that transfers

ownership of real property from one person to another; in family law, deeds are often used to transfer a marital home as part of property division in a divorce.
Explanation: A paper that proves the transfer of ownership of land or a house.
Example: The divorce decree required the husband to sign a deed transferring the family home to the wife.

DEFAULT
Definition: A party's failure to file a timely response after valid service. Entry of default prevents that party from participating unless the default is set aside, but the court must still review the requesting party's evidence and may not grant relief beyond the notice and requests permitted by law.
Explanation: If the respondent does not respond on time, the petitioner may ask to proceed by default, but the judge must still determine whether the requested orders are legally supported.
Example: After the respondent failed to file a Response, the petitioner submitted the required default documents and evidence for the court's review.
See also: DEFAULT JUDGMENT; RELIEF FROM DEFAULT.

DEFAULT JUDGMENT
Definition: A court decision entered against a party who fails to respond or appear in the case.
Explanation: The judge's decision when someone doesn't show up or answer.
Example: The court entered a default judgment in the divorce case.
See also: DEFAULT.

DEFER
Definition: To postpone or delay a court action, decision, or obligation to a later time, usually by judicial discretion; in family law, deferral may apply to hearings, payments, or enforcement of orders when circumstances justify a temporary delay.
Explanation: When the judge or court puts off a decision or action until later.
Example: The judge chose to defer ruling on child support until the custody evaluation was complete.

DEFINED BENEFIT PLAN

Definition: A retirement plan that promises a monthly benefit based on a formula such as salary, age, and years of service. In divorce, the community share may be divided by a domestic relations order, and issues may include retirement timing, survivor benefits, and postseparation benefit increases.
Explanation: This type of pension pays a formula based monthly amount, often for life.
Example: The parties used a time rule formula to divide the community share of Wife's county pension.
See also: BROWN TIME RULE; GILLMORE ELECTION; LEHMAN PENSION ENHANCEMENT RULE.

DEFINED CONTRIBUTION PLAN

Definition: A retirement plan with an individual account whose value depends on contributions and investment results, such as a 401(k), 403(b), or many profit sharing plans. A divorce order may divide the account and related gains or losses as of a stated date.
Explanation: This type of retirement plan has an account balance that rises or falls with deposits and investments.
Example: The QDRO awarded Husband one half of the community portion of Wife's 401(k), plus gains and losses until transfer.
See also: QUALIFIED DOMESTIC RELATIONS ORDER (QDRO); SEPARATE INTEREST QDRO.

DEPARTMENT OF CHILD SUPPORT SERVICES (DCSS)

Definition: A governmental child support agency that establishes, enforces, modifies, collects, and distributes support obligations as authorized by law.
Explanation: The state office that makes sure child support is paid.
Example: DCSS began enforcement proceedings against the father.
See also: LOCAL CHILD SUPPORT AGENCY (LCSA); STATE DISBURSEMENT UNIT (SDU).

DEPENDENCY

Definition: A juvenile court proceeding and legal status under which a child is found to come within Welfare and Institutions Code §300 because of abuse, neglect, abandonment, or another statutory basis, and the juvenile court assumes protective jurisdiction.
Explanation: The juvenile court protects and supervises a child after

making the required statutory findings.
Example: The juvenile court declared the child a dependent of the court after sustaining the section 300 petition.
See also: ABUSE - CHILD.

DEPONENT
Definition: A person who gives sworn testimony in writing or orally outside of court, usually during a deposition, in response to questions; in family law, deponents may include parties, witnesses, or experts.
Explanation: Someone who answers questions under oath before trial.
Example: The mother became a deponent when she gave sworn answers in a deposition about custody.

DEPOSE
Definition: To question a witness or party under oath outside of court, usually in a deposition, for the purpose of gathering testimony and evidence; in family law, parties may be deposed about finances, custody, or conduct.
Explanation: To ask someone questions under oath before the trial.
Example: The father's attorney moved to depose the custody evaluator about her report.

DEPOSITION
Definition: A formal session where a witness or party gives sworn testimony outside of court, recorded by a court reporter, to be used as evidence or for discovery; in family law, depositions often cover income, parenting ability, or allegations of abuse.
Explanation: A meeting where someone answers questions under oath before trial, and the answers are written down.
Example: The father gave a deposition about his income and work history for the child support case.
See also: DISCOVERY.

DEPOSITION SUBPOENA FOR BUSINESS RECORDS
Definition: A discovery subpoena requiring a nonparty business, employer, bank, school, medical provider, or other records holder to produce documents. California notice, service, privacy, and consumer objection rules may apply before records can be released.
Explanation: A party uses a subpoena to obtain records from someone who is not a party to the case.

Example: Mother served a records subpoena on Father's employer for payroll and bonus records after giving the required consumer notice.

DESERTION

Definition: The intentional abandonment of a spouse or child. California is a no fault dissolution state, so desertion is not a required ground for divorce, although abandonment-related facts may be relevant to support, custody, adoption, dependency, or proceedings concerning parental rights.

Explanation: Leaving a spouse or child may have legal consequences, but a California divorce does not require proof of desertion.

Example: The spouse sought dissolution based on irreconcilable differences and separately raised the other parent's prolonged absence in the custody proceeding.

DIRECT EVIDENCE

Definition: Evidence that directly proves a fact without requiring inference, such as eyewitness testimony or an admission; in family law, direct evidence might include testimony about an incident of abuse.

Explanation: Proof that directly shows a fact happened.

Example: The child's testimony that he witnessed violence was direct evidence in the custody case.

See also: EVIDENCE.

DIRECT EXAMINATION

Definition: The initial questioning of a witness by the attorney who called them to testify, intended to present evidence in support of that party's case; in family law, direct examination may involve testimony about parenting ability or financial needs.

Explanation: When a lawyer questions their own witness first in court.

Example: On direct examination, the mother described the daily routine she provides for the child.

See also: CROSS EXAMINATION; REDIRECT EXAMINATION; EXAMINATION (DIRECT AND CROSS).

DIRECT TRACING / FAMILY EXPENSE PRESUMPTION

Definition: A method for proving that property or a payment came from separate funds by following the money through records. California also generally presumes that available community funds were used first for ordinary family expenses, which can affect whether separate funds

remained available for a later purchase.
Explanation: Good records may trace separate money, but normal family bills are usually treated as paid from community funds first.
Example: Bank records showed that Wife's inheritance remained in the account and directly funded the down payment after community income paid the household bills.
See also: COMMINGLING.

DISABLED
Definition: A person may have a physical or mental disability that is protected or otherwise recognized by law. Disability is not a single legal status, and in a custody case the court must consider the person's actual parenting abilities, available supports, and the effect, if any, on the child rather than relying on the diagnosis alone.
Explanation: A disability may require accommodation, but the court should evaluate actual abilities and needs rather than stereotypes.
Example: The court provided an accessible hearing and evaluated the parent's actual caregiving plan without assuming that the disability made the parent unfit.
DISAGREEMENT
Definition: A conflict or difference of opinion between parties regarding facts, rights, or obligations; in family law, disagreements often concern custody, visitation schedules, or financial support.
Explanation: When the parties do not agree about an issue in court.
Example: A disagreement over the child's school choice led to a contested custody hearing.

DISCOVERY
Definition: The pretrial process through which parties exchange information and evidence relevant to the case, including depositions, interrogatories, document requests, and admissions; in family law, discovery helps determine financial status, parenting ability, or allegations of abuse.
Explanation: The process of gathering and sharing information before trial.
Example: Through discovery, the mother obtained the father's bank records for the child support case.
See also: FORM INTERROGATORIES; REQUEST FOR PRODUCTION; DEPOSITION.

DISCOVERY SANCTIONS

Definition: Penalties for misusing or refusing discovery, such as failing to answer questions, produce records, obey a discovery order, or meet and confer in good faith. Sanctions may include money, limits on evidence, established facts, dismissal, default, or contempt, depending on the violation.

Explanation: The court may punish a party who blocks the fair exchange of information before trial.

Example: After Husband ignored two production orders, the court ordered monetary sanctions and barred him from using undisclosed bank records at trial.

See also: MOTION TO COMPEL.

DISMISSAL

Definition: A court's termination of a case without further hearing or judgment; in family law, dismissal may occur if the petition is withdrawn, settled, or legally insufficient.

Explanation: When the court ends a case before a final decision.

Example: The judge granted a dismissal of the custody petition after the parties reconciled.

DISMISSAL WITH PREJUDICE

Definition: A dismissal that generally bars the same cause of action or claim from being filed again. In family law, however, many custody and support orders remain modifiable when the governing statutes permit later relief based on changed circumstances, so the effect of "with prejudice" depends on what was dismissed.

Explanation: The dismissed claim usually cannot be refiled, but the phrase does not eliminate statutory power to modify future family law orders when the law allows it.

Example: The related civil claim was dismissed with prejudice as part of the settlement and could not be filed again.

DISMISSAL WITHOUT PREJUDICE

Definition: A court's termination of a case that allows the petitioner to refile the same claim in the future; in family law, dismissals without prejudice often occur when a petition is incomplete or premature.

Explanation: When the court ends a case but allows it to be filed again later.

Example: The father's child support petition was dismissed without prejudice so he could refile with proper documentation.

DISPENSE WITH

Definition: To waive or eliminate a legal requirement, procedure, or formality by court order; in family law, courts may dispense with notice, service, or consent under certain circumstances.

Explanation: When the court says a normal legal step is not needed.

Example: The judge decided to dispense with the father's consent to the adoption due to abandonment.

DISPOSITION

Definition: The court's final determination of a case or a specific issue within a case; in family law, disposition may include custody orders, support determinations, or findings of dependency.

Explanation: The final decision the court makes in a case.

Example: The disposition of the divorce case awarded custody to the mother and child support from the father.

DISPOSITION OF ASSETS

Definition: The allocation, sale, or transfer of property as determined by court order or agreement; in family law, it refers to how marital or community assets are divided at divorce.

Explanation: How the court decides property or money will be handled in divorce.

Example: The judge ordered the disposition of assets by dividing the marital home and retirement accounts.

DISPOSITIONAL HEARING

Definition: A hearing held after a finding of dependency, neglect, or delinquency to determine the appropriate placement, custody, or services for a child; in family law, dispositional hearings focus on the child's best interests and long term plan.

Explanation: A court hearing to decide what should happen to a child after the court finds abuse, neglect, or dependency.

Example: At the dispositional hearing, the judge ordered foster care and reunification services for the parents.

DISSOLUTION OF MARRIAGE

Definition: The judicial process that legally ends a valid marriage and resolves related custody, support, and property issues.

Explanation: Another word for divorce; ending a marriage legally.
Example: She filed a petition for dissolution of marriage.

DISTURBING THE PEACE
Definition: A form of abuse under California's Domestic Violence Prevention Act that destroys another person's mental or emotional calm. It can include harassment, threats, repeated unwanted contact, coercive control, impersonation, or abuse through electronic accounts and connected devices.
Explanation: Domestic violence can include conduct that seriously disrupts a person's safety and peace of mind, even without physical injury.
Example: The court found that hundreds of threatening messages and account intrusions disturbed the protected party's peace.
See also: DOMESTIC VIOLENCE.

DIVORCE
Definition: The legal dissolution of a valid marriage by a court, terminating the marital relationship and addressing related issues such as custody, visitation, child support, spousal support, and division of property.
Explanation: When a court officially ends a marriage and decides custody, support, and property matters.
Example: The court granted the divorce and ordered joint legal custody of the children.

DNA
Definition: Deoxyribonucleic acid, the genetic material used for identification; in family law, DNA testing is often used to establish or dispute paternity and parentage, providing nearly conclusive evidence of biological relationships.
Explanation: Genetic testing used to prove if someone is the biological parent of a child.
Example: The court ordered DNA testing to confirm the alleged father's paternity.
See also: PATERNITY.

DOCKET
Definition: The official list or calendar of cases maintained by a court, showing scheduled hearings, filings, and pending matters; in family law,

the docket includes divorce, custody, support, and protection cases.
Explanation: The court's official list of all the cases it must handle.
Example: The divorce case appeared on the family court's docket for hearing next month.

DOCKET NUMBER
Definition: A unique identifying number assigned by the court to each case, used for tracking filings, orders, and proceedings; in family law, docket numbers ensure accurate reference to divorce, custody, or support cases.
Explanation: The special number given to each case to keep track of it in court.
Example: The custody petition was filed under docket number BFL 25 123456.

DOCUMENTARY PROOF
Definition: Written or recorded evidence submitted to the court to establish a fact, such as contracts, financial records, medical reports, or school records; in family law, documentary proof supports claims regarding income, parenting ability, or allegations of abuse.
Explanation: Written or recorded documents used as evidence in court.
Example: The mother presented documentary proof of the father's income through his pay stubs.
See also: EVIDENCE.

DOMESTIC RELATIONS ORDER (DRO)
Definition: A court order that assigns rights in retirement benefits to a spouse, former spouse, child, or other dependent. A DRO becomes a qualified domestic relations order, or QDRO, only if it meets federal requirements for a covered private retirement plan; government plans may use different order types.
Explanation: It is the retirement division order. The exact form depends on the retirement plan.
Example: The court entered a DRO dividing the state pension, while a separate QDRO divided the private 401(k).
See also: QUALIFIED DOMESTIC RELATIONS ORDER (QDRO); JOINDER (INCLUDING RETIREMENT PLAN JOINDER).

DOMESTIC VIOLENCE
Definition: Abuse against a person protected by California's Domestic

Violence Prevention Act. It may include physical injury, sexual assault, threats, stalking, harassment, destroying property, disturbing the peace, coercive control, reproductive coercion, and other conduct described by statute, even when no physical injury occurs.
Explanation: Domestic violence can be physical or nonphysical conduct used to harm, threaten, harass, isolate, monitor, or control a protected person.
Example: The court issued a restraining order after evidence of domestic violence.
See also: COERCIVE CONTROL; DISTURBING THE PEACE; DOMESTIC VIOLENCE RESTRAINING ORDER; BATTERER INTERVENTION PROGRAM (BIP).

DOMESTIC VIOLENCE RESTRAINING ORDER
Definition: A court order that protects a person from abuse, threats, or harassment by a current or former spouse, partner, family member, or household member. It can restrict contact, require the abuser to move out, and provide temporary custody or support orders.
Explanation: A legal order to keep an abuser away from the victim and protect their safety.
Example: The judge issued a domestic violence restraining order preventing the husband from contacting his wife and children.
See also: DOMESTIC VIOLENCE; TEMPORARY RESTRAINING ORDER; FINAL RESTRAINING ORDER; DVRO RENEWAL / RITCHIE STANDARD; FIREARMS RELINQUISHMENT ORDER.

DOMESTIC VIOLENCE RISK ASSESSMENT
Definition: An evaluation used to assess the likelihood of domestic violence occurring or recurring, often used in custody or protective order cases.
Explanation: A test to see how likely domestic violence is to happen or happen again.
Example: The court required a domestic violence risk assessment before allowing unsupervised visitation.

DOMICILE
Definition: A person's permanent legal home, established by physical presence and intent to remain or return. Domicile may affect dissolution jurisdiction and other legal questions, but interstate child custody jurisdiction is governed primarily by the UCCJEA, including the child's

home state, rather than by a parent's domicile alone.
Explanation: A person's true home for legal purposes, not just where they are temporarily staying.
Example: The court considered domicile and statutory residence requirements in determining whether it had jurisdiction to enter a dissolution judgment.

DONOR NOT A PARENT

Definition: A parentage rule that a sperm or egg donor is generally not a legal parent when the donation is made under California's assisted reproduction laws. The result can depend on the method used, the written agreement, the parties' intent, and whether a statutory exception applies.
Explanation: A person who provides sperm or eggs for assisted reproduction usually does not become a legal parent when the law's requirements are met.
Example: The known sperm donor had no parental rights because the written assisted reproduction agreement stated that the intended parents would be the child's only parents.
See also: ASSISTED REPRODUCTION; INTENDED PARENT.

DUE DILIGENCE

Definition: The reasonable efforts a person must make to fulfill a legal requirement or obligation; in family law, due diligence often arises when attempting service of process, investigating financial records, or locating a missing parent.
Explanation: Taking all reasonable steps to meet a legal responsibility.
Example: The petitioner showed due diligence in trying to serve the father with custody papers before requesting service by publication.

DUE PROCESS

Definition: The constitutional guarantee that legal proceedings will be fair, that individuals will receive notice of proceedings, and that they will have an opportunity to be heard; in family law, due process ensures fairness in custody, support, and parental rights cases.
Explanation: The right to fair legal procedures, including notice and a chance to be heard.
Example: The father argued that his due process rights were violated when the custody hearing was held without notifying him.

DUE PROCESS OF LAW

Definition: A broader legal principle that incorporates both procedural due process (fair procedures) and substantive due process (protection of fundamental rights), ensuring justice and fairness in court proceedings; in family law, it applies in termination of parental rights, custody determinations, and adoption cases.

Explanation: The legal rule that courts must act fairly and protect basic rights when making decisions.

Example: The appellate court reversed the termination of parental rights because the parents were denied due process of law.

DURESS

Definition: Unlawful pressure or coercion that forces someone to act against their free will, such as signing an agreement; in family law, a divorce settlement or prenuptial agreement signed under duress may be invalid.

Explanation: When someone is forced or pressured to do something they don't want to do, making it unfair.

Example: The wife argued that she signed the marital settlement agreement under duress.

DUTY

Definition: A legal obligation to act or refrain from acting in a certain way; in family law, duties include the duty to support children financially, to provide care, or to comply with court orders.

Explanation: A legal responsibility that a person must follow.

Example: Parents have a legal duty to provide financial support for their children.

DVRO RENEWAL / RITCHIE STANDARD

Definition: The standard for renewing a domestic violence restraining order. New abuse is not required. Under Family Code §6345 and Ritchie v. Konrad, the protected person must generally show an objectively reasonable fear that future abuse may occur if the order ends.

Explanation: A DVRO may be renewed without a new incident when the protected person's fear of future abuse is reasonable.

Example: The court permanently renewed the order based on the prior violence, continued blame, and credible fear of renewed contact.

See also: DOMESTIC VIOLENCE RESTRAINING ORDER.

EARLY NEUTRAL EVALUATION (FAMILY LAW)

Definition: A process where a neutral evaluator listens to both parties early in the case and provides an assessment to encourage settlement.
Explanation: An early review by a neutral expert to help settle the case.
Example: The parties participated in early neutral evaluation to avoid a trial.

ELISOR ORDER

Definition: An enforcement order authorizing the court clerk or another named person to sign a deed, retirement order, release, or other document when a party refuses or fails to sign as ordered. The order carries out an existing duty; it does not create a new agreement for the refusing party.
Explanation: The court can appoint someone else to sign a required document when a party will not cooperate.
Example: After Husband ignored repeated orders to sign the grant deed, the court appointed the clerk as elisor to sign it.

ELKINS HEARING

Definition: Common California family law shorthand for a hearing with live, admissible evidence under principles from Elkins v. Superior Court and Family Code § 217. The court ordinarily should not decide disputed facts only from written declarations when live testimony is required and properly requested.
Explanation: The parties present witnesses and evidence in court instead of relying only on written statements.
Example: The judge set an Elkins hearing so both parents and the custody evaluator could testify and be cross examined.

EMANCIPATION

Definition: A legal process by which a minor is declared independent from parental control and responsibility.
Explanation: A teenager is made legally independent from their parents.
Example: She sought emancipation to live on her own before age 18.

EMERGENCY CUSTODY ORDER

Definition: A temporary custody order issued on an expedited basis to protect a child from immediate harm or removal.
Explanation: A fast custody order when a child is unsafe.
Example: The judge signed an emergency custody order after the abuse

report.

EMERGENCY PROTECTIVE ORDER (EPO)
Definition: A very short term protective order issued by a judicial officer at the request of a law enforcement officer when immediate protection is needed. An EPO may address domestic violence, stalking, child abuse, child abduction, elder abuse, or other qualifying emergencies and ordinarily remains in effect only long enough for the protected person to seek a longer court order.
Explanation: A police officer asks an on call judicial officer for an immediate order to protect a person until regular court relief can be requested.
Example: After responding to the domestic violence call, the officer requested and obtained an emergency protective order from the on call judicial officer.

EMERGENCY RELIEF
Definition: Immediate, temporary orders issued by the court to protect parties or children from harm or to preserve the status quo until a full hearing can be held; in family law, emergency relief may include restraining orders, temporary custody, or suspension of visitation.
Explanation: Quick court action to protect someone until a full hearing can happen.
Example: The judge granted emergency relief by giving the mother temporary custody after evidence of abuse.

EMERGENCY TEMPORARY CUSTODY
Definition: A temporary custody order granted by the court when a child is in immediate danger or urgent action is required.
Explanation: A short term custody order to protect a child in danger.
Example: The grandmother was granted emergency temporary custody after allegations of neglect arose.

EMPLOYER
Definition: A person or entity that hires and pays workers; in family law, employers are often directed by court order to withhold child support or spousal support payments directly from an employee's wages.
Explanation: A person or company that gives someone a job and pays them.
Example: The father's employer was ordered to deduct child support

payments from his paycheck.

ENFORCE
Definition: To compel compliance with a law, order, or judgment through legal means; in family law, courts enforce child support, spousal support, custody, and visitation orders through contempt, wage garnishment, or other remedies.
Explanation: To make sure a court order is obeyed.
Example: The court moved to enforce the visitation order after repeated violations by the mother.

ENFORCEABLE BY THE COURT
Definition: A right, duty, or agreement that can be compelled or upheld by legal action; in family law, agreements regarding custody, support, or property division must be enforceable by the court to carry legal weight.
Explanation: Something the judge can make happen by law.
Example: The parenting agreement became enforceable by the court once it was signed by the judge.

ENFORCEMENT
Definition: The legal process of ensuring compliance with a court order or judgment; in family law, enforcement actions include garnishment of wages, contempt findings, or suspension of licenses for nonpayment of support.
Explanation: Steps taken to make sure court orders are followed.
Example: The state child support agency initiated enforcement after months of unpaid support.

ENJOIN
Definition: To legally prohibit or command an act through a court order, often issued as an injunction; in family law, courts may enjoin harassment, removal of children from jurisdiction, or dissipation of marital assets.
Explanation: When the judge orders someone to stop doing or to do something.
Example: The court enjoined the father from taking the child out of state without permission.

ENTER AN ORDER
Definition: The formal act by which a court's decision is recorded as an

official order, making it legally binding and enforceable.
Explanation: When the judge officially records a decision as a court order.
Example: The judge entered an order granting joint custody of the children.

ENTERTAIN A MOTION
Definition: To consider and rule upon a motion submitted by a party; in family law, judges entertain motions on issues such as temporary custody, child support, visitation, or protective orders.
Explanation: When a judge agrees to hear and decide on a request made in a case.
Example: The court agreed to entertain a motion for temporary child support during the divorce.

ENTRY OF JUDGMENT
Definition: The recording of a final judgment in the official court record, making it effective and enforceable; in family law, this may include divorce decrees, custody judgments, or support orders.
Explanation: When the final decision of the court is officially entered into the record.
Example: The clerk filed the entry of judgment for the divorce, finalizing the case.
See also: JUDGMENT.

EPSTEIN CREDITS
Definition: A reimbursement credit given to a spouse in a divorce case for separate property funds used to pay community debts after separation. It comes from the California case In re Marriage of Epstein (1979).
Explanation: A spouse gets credit when they use their own money (not community funds) to pay off joint debts after separation.
Example: The wife received Epstein credits for paying the mortgage with her separate earnings after the couple separated.
See also: WATTS CHARGES; BRANCO CREDITS; JEFFRIES CREDITS.

EQUAL PROTECTION OF LAWS
Definition: A constitutional principle under the Fourteenth Amendment requiring that similarly situated individuals be treated equally under the

law; in family law, equal protection may apply to custody rights, adoption eligibility, or support obligations.
Explanation: The rule that people in the same situation must be treated the same by law.
Example: The father argued that denying him custody rights violated equal protection of laws.

EQUALIZATION PAYMENT
Definition: Money ordered or agreed to be paid by one spouse to the other to make the overall division of community property equal. It is often used when one spouse keeps an asset that cannot be divided easily, such as a home, vehicle, or business.
Explanation: One spouse pays cash so each spouse receives the same net value from the property division.
Example: Wife kept the family home and paid Husband a $75,000 equalization payment for his share of the equity.
See also: ASSET DIVISION; BUYOUT (MARITAL HOME BUYOUT).

EQUITABLE DISTRIBUTION
Definition: A property division system used in many noncommunity property states, under which marital property is divided fairly rather than necessarily equally. California instead generally requires equal division of the community estate unless a statute or valid agreement provides otherwise.
Explanation: Other states may divide marital property equitably; California generally divides community property equally.
Example: A court in an equitable distribution state divided marital property under that state's fairness factors, while a California court would ordinarily begin with equal division of the community estate.

ESTATE
Definition: All property, assets, and debts owned by a person at death, or sometimes during life in trust or guardianship; in family law, estates are relevant in cases of inheritance, child support claims against estates, or guardianship of a child's estate.
Explanation: Everything a person owns, including money, property, and debts, especially after death.
Example: The child's guardian was appointed to manage the estate inherited from his grandparents.

EVIDENCE
Definition: Testimony, documents, objects, or other items presented to the court to prove or disprove facts in dispute; in family law, evidence may include school records, financial statements, medical reports, or witness testimony concerning custody, support, or abuse.
Explanation: Proof presented in court to show whether something is true.
Example: The mother presented evidence of the father's missed child support payments at the hearing.
See also: ADMISSIBILITY; CIRCUMSTANTIAL EVIDENCE; DIRECT EVIDENCE; DOCUMENTARY PROOF.

EVIDENCE CODE SECTION 352 OBJECTION
Definition: The rule allowing a judge to exclude relevant evidence when its value is substantially outweighed by undue use of time or a substantial danger of unfair prejudice, confusing the issues, or misleading the factfinder. It is often called a Section 352 objection.
Explanation: The judge may keep out evidence that causes too much unfair harm, delay, or confusion compared with what it proves.
Example: The court excluded graphic photographs under Section 352 because less disturbing evidence proved the same point.
See also: EVIDENCE CODE SECTIONS 350/351 - RELEVANCE; MOTION IN LIMINE.

EVIDENCE CODE SECTION 403 OBJECTION
Definition: The rule used when evidence is admissible only if another fact is first shown, such as identity, authenticity, personal knowledge, or a connection to the case. The proponent must offer enough evidence for the judge or factfinder to find that preliminary fact.
Explanation: Before the evidence can be used, the party must first show why it is genuine or connected to the case.
Example: The text message screenshots were excluded until Mother offered evidence linking the number and account to Father.
See also: EVIDENCE CODE SECTION 1400 OBJECTION; CHAIN OF CUSTODY.

EVIDENCE CODE SECTION 702 OBJECTION
Definition: The rule that a witness generally may testify only about matters the witness personally perceived, unless the witness is giving a proper expert opinion. The objection is commonly stated as lack of

personal knowledge.
Explanation: A witness must usually have seen, heard, or otherwise perceived the fact personally.
Example: The court sustained a Section 702 objection when the witness tried to describe a custody exchange that happened while she was not present.
See also: EVIDENCE CODE SECTION 800 OBJECTION; EXPERT TESTIMONY.

EVIDENCE CODE SECTION 800 OBJECTION
Definition: The rule limiting a nonexpert witness's opinions to those based on the witness's own perceptions and helpful to understanding the testimony. A lay witness usually may not give medical diagnoses, complex property values, or expert custody opinions.
Explanation: A regular witness may give a useful common sense opinion based on what the witness personally observed, but not a technical expert opinion.
Example: The teacher could describe the child's behavior but could not diagnose the child with an anxiety disorder.
See also: EVIDENCE CODE SECTION 702 OBJECTION.

EVIDENCE CODE SECTION 1200 - HEARSAY
Definition: The rule excluding an out of court statement offered to prove that what the statement says is true, unless an exception or exclusion applies. A statement offered for another relevant purpose, such as notice or effect on the listener, may not be hearsay.
Explanation: A witness usually cannot repeat someone else's statement to prove the statement was true unless a legal exception applies.
Example: The court sustained a hearsay objection when Mother repeated what an absent neighbor said about Father.
See also: HEARSAY.

EVIDENCE CODE SECTION 1400 OBJECTION
Definition: The requirement that a party offer enough evidence to support a finding that a writing, photograph, recording, message, or other item is what the party claims it is. Authentication can come from a witness, distinctive details, metadata, admissions, or other evidence.
Explanation: The party must show that the evidence is genuine before the judge relies on it.
Example: Mother authenticated the messages by identifying Father's

number, writing style, and references to facts only he knew.
See also: EVIDENCE CODE SECTION 403 OBJECTION.

EVIDENCE CODE SECTIONS 350/351 - RELEVANCE
Definition: The basic rules that irrelevant evidence is inadmissible and relevant evidence is generally admissible unless another law excludes it. Evidence is relevant when it has any reasonable tendency to prove or disprove an important disputed fact.
Explanation: Evidence must help answer an issue the judge actually has to decide.
Example: The court excluded testimony about a parent's college dating history because it did not help decide the present custody issues.
See also: EVIDENCE CODE SECTION 352 OBJECTION.

EVIDENTIARY HEARING
Definition: A court proceeding in which parties present admissible evidence and testimony for factual findings and a ruling.
Explanation: A hearing where the judge listens to evidence from both sides.
Example: The court scheduled an evidentiary hearing on visitation issues.

EX PARTE MOTION
Definition: A request for temporary emergency or other permitted relief presented on shortened notice. In California family law, notice to the other party is generally required unless the court waives notice under exceptional circumstances; "ex parte" does not automatically mean that the other side receives no notice.
Explanation: The court considers an urgent request quickly, usually after shortened notice to the other side.
Example: She gave the required emergency notice and filed an ex parte request for temporary custody based on immediate safety concerns.

EX PARTE ORDER
Definition: A temporary order issued on an emergency or other authorized ex parte request before a regularly noticed hearing. The opposing party may receive shortened notice and an opportunity to respond, and notice may be excused only when the governing rule permits.
Explanation: It is a fast temporary order, often made after shortened

notice and followed by a fuller hearing.
Example: The court issued a temporary emergency custody order and set a prompt noticed hearing.

EXAMINATION (DIRECT AND CROSS)
Definition: Questioning of witnesses in court, either by the party who called them (direct) or the opposing party (cross).
Explanation: When lawyers ask questions of witnesses in court.
Example: The father's attorney conducted a cross examination of the witness.
See also: DIRECT EXAMINATION.

EXCLUSIVE CONTINUING JURISDICTION - UCCJEA
Definition: The rule that the state making a valid child custody determination generally keeps control over later custody changes until statutory conditions show that the child and parents no longer have the required connection or that they no longer live in that state.
Explanation: The state that properly made the custody order usually keeps the case until the legal connection to that state ends.
Example: California kept exclusive continuing jurisdiction because one parent and the child still lived here and important evidence remained here.
See also: UNIFORM CHILD CUSTODY JURISDICTION AND ENFORCEMENT ACT (UCCJEA).

EXECUTION AGAINST WAGES
Definition: A court ordered process directing an employer to withhold a portion of an employee's wages to satisfy a judgment or debt; in family law, commonly used to collect overdue child support or spousal support.
Explanation: When the court orders money to be taken directly from a person's paycheck to pay support.
Example: The judge ordered execution against wages after the father fell behind on child support.
See also: WAGE GARNISHMENT.

EXEMPT
Definition: Legally protected from a particular duty, calculation, levy, or enforcement remedy. Whether income or property is exempt depends on the specific statute and purpose; disability related payments are not all treated the same for support or collection.
Explanation: When something is legally excused from a rule or

payment.
Example: The court examined the source of the disability benefit and the governing statute before deciding whether it counted as support income or was protected from enforcement.

EXEMPTION

Definition: A specific exclusion or privilege that removes a person or property from liability or obligation under the law; in family law, exemptions may include child tax exemptions or statutory exemptions in calculating income for support.
Explanation: A rule that allows someone to avoid paying or being subject to something the law usually requires.
Example: The mother claimed the child as a tax exemption after being awarded primary custody.

EXHIBIT

Definition: A document, record, object, or piece of evidence formally introduced in court proceedings to support a party's case; in family law, exhibits may include school records, medical reports, pay stubs, or photographs.
Explanation: A piece of evidence shown to the judge in court.
Example: The mother introduced the child's medical records as an exhibit in the custody trial.

EXPEDITED ENFORCEMENT - UCCJEA

Definition: A fast court procedure for enforcing another state's registered or enforceable custody order. The court may order the respondent to appear with the child on the next judicial day unless a later date is necessary, and only limited defenses are allowed.
Explanation: A parent can ask for a quick hearing to enforce a custody order from another state.
Example: The court set a next day UCCJEA enforcement hearing and ordered Father to bring the child and the out of state order.
See also: REGISTRATION OF OUT OF STATE CUSTODY ORDER.

EXPENSES

Definition: The costs or outlays incurred by parties in relation to a legal matter; in family law, expenses often include child care, medical costs, educational costs, and litigation expenses.
Explanation: Money spent on needs or related costs, sometimes shared

by the parents.
Example: The decree required both parents to share the child's extracurricular expenses equally.

EXPERT TESTIMONY
Definition: Evidence given by a qualified professional who provides specialized knowledge to assist the court in understanding complex issues; in family law, expert testimony may involve psychologists, financial analysts, or child development specialists.
Explanation: When a professional explains technical or specialized matters to the court.
Example: The court relied on expert testimony from a psychologist about the child's attachment to each parent.
See also: EVIDENCE CODE SECTION 702 OBJECTION.

EXPERT WITNESS
Definition: A professional with specialized expertise who is qualified by the court to give opinions and testify about matters requiring expert knowledge; in family law, expert witnesses often include custody evaluators, accountants, and medical professionals.
Explanation: A professional allowed by the judge to give expert opinions in court.
Example: The custody evaluator testified as an expert witness in the relocation case.

EXPERT WITNESS EXCHANGE
Definition: The formal pretrial disclosure of expert witnesses, their qualifications, expected opinions, and supporting reports or writings when required by the discovery statutes or a court order. Missing the deadline may lead to exclusion of the expert's testimony.
Explanation: Each side identifies its experts and opinions before trial so there are no unfair surprises.
Example: The court excluded a late valuation expert because the party did not include the expert in the ordered exchange.

EXTEND
Definition: To lengthen the time period or expand the scope of a court order, obligation, or deadline; in family law, courts may extend restraining orders, support obligations, or deadlines for filing.
Explanation: To make something last longer or cover more time.

Example: The judge extended the temporary restraining order for another six months.

EXTENSION

Definition: The act of granting additional time to perform a legal duty or the continuation of a court order; in family law, extensions may apply to visitation periods, filing deadlines, or temporary orders.
Explanation: Extra time given to meet a deadline or continue an order.
Example: The father requested an extension to file his financial disclosure in the divorce case.

EXTENUATING CIRCUMSTANCES

Definition: Facts or conditions that lessen the severity or culpability of an act, often considered by courts when determining consequences; in family law, extenuating circumstances may justify missed payments, visitation issues, or delays.
Explanation: Special conditions that help explain or excuse someone's failure to follow an order.
Example: The court considered extenuating circumstances when the mother missed visitation due to hospitalization.

EYEWITNESS

Definition: A person who directly observes and testifies about an event relevant to the case; in family law, eyewitness testimony may relate to parenting practices, domestic violence, or child neglect.
Explanation: Someone who saw what happened and tells about it.
Example: An eyewitness testified that the father struck the mother during a visitation exchange.

FACTUAL BASIS

Definition: The underlying facts and evidence that support a claim, order, or legal conclusion; in family law, courts require a factual basis to issue orders regarding custody, support, or termination of parental rights.
Explanation: The facts that back up a court's decision or a party's claim.
Example: The judge found a factual basis for terminating parental rights due to continued neglect.

FAMILY CASE CONFERENCE

Definition: A meeting between the parties, their lawyers, and sometimes a judge or mediator to discuss family law issues and encourage settlement

before trial.
Explanation: A meeting to talk about family law issues and try to settle before going to trial.
Example: The judge scheduled a family case conference to resolve custody and support disputes.

FAMILY COURT

Definition: The part of a California superior court that handles family law matters, including dissolution, legal separation, parentage, custody, support, and domestic violence proceedings. It is a division or assignment within the superior court, not a separate statewide court system.
Explanation: In California, family law cases are heard in the family law division or departments of the superior court.
Example: Their custody dispute was assigned to a family law department of the superior court.

FAMILY COURT SERVICES

Definition: Court connected programs providing mediation, custody counseling, evaluations, and related assistance in family disputes involving children.
Explanation: Services run by the court to help with custody cases.
Example: They attended mediation through family court services.
See also: CHILD CUSTODY RECOMMENDING COUNSELING (CCRC).

FAMILY COURT SERVICES REPORT

Definition: A written report prepared by Family Court Services, often after mediation or investigation, giving recommendations to the judge about custody or visitation.
Explanation: A report from family court staff with recommendations about custody or visitation.
Example: The family court services report recommended joint custody with the mother as the primary caregiver.

FAMILY DIVISION

Definition: A branch or group of departments within a superior court assigned to family law matters. The precise organization varies by county; juvenile dependency and delinquency are generally handled in juvenile court, and some adoption or guardianship matters may be assigned under

local court structure.
Explanation: It is the part of the superior court assigned to family law cases, with local differences in how related matters are organized.
Example: The custody petition was filed in the family division of the superior court, where judges focus on family law matters.

FAMILY LAW ATTORNEY'S REAL PROPERTY LIEN (FLARPL)
Definition: A lien under Family Code §2033 against a party's interest in community real property to secure payment of family law attorney's fees. The attorney must give advance notice, and the client or other party may object and obtain an expedited hearing.
Explanation: A family law attorney may secure unpaid fees with a lien on the client's share of community real estate, but special notice rules apply.
Example: Counsel served the required notice before recording a FLARPL against the client's community interest in the home.
See also: ATTORNEY'S FEES AND COSTS.

FAMILY LAW FACILITATOR
Definition: A court employee who helps self represented parties with forms and procedures in family law cases.
Explanation: A helper at court who explains family law paperwork.
Example: The family law facilitator helped him complete the child support forms.

FAMILY MEDIATION AGREEMENT
Definition: A written settlement reached by parties in mediation, often covering custody, visitation, and support, which can be made into a court order.
Explanation: The written agreement parents make in mediation about custody and support.
Example: The parents signed a family mediation agreement resolving all custody issues.

FAMILY REUNIFICATION
Definition: The process of returning children in foster care to their parents when safe and appropriate.
Explanation: Sending foster children back to their parents safely.
Example: The agency developed a plan for family reunification.

FAMILY SUPPORT
Definition: Financial assistance ordered by the court that combines both child support and spousal support into a single payment; commonly used in jurisdictions where calculating one combined obligation simplifies enforcement and collection.
Explanation: A court ordered payment that covers both child support and spousal support together.
Example: The divorce decree required the father to pay monthly family support, which included money for the children and the ex spouse.
See also: CHILD SUPPORT; SPOUSAL SUPPORT.

FATHER'S RIGHTS
Definition: The parental rights and responsibilities of a person who is legally established as a father. California does not create a separate gender based custody standard for fathers; once parentage is established, custody and parenting time are determined under the same statutes and the child's best interests.
Explanation: A legally established father may seek custody and parenting time under the same best interest standards applied to other parents.
Example: After parentage was established, the father requested a parenting plan under the same custody statutes governing both parents.

FEE SCHEDULE
Definition: A detailed list of the costs and charges set by law or the court for filing documents, motions, or other legal services; in family law, fee schedules govern filing fees for divorce petitions, custody motions, and certified copies.
Explanation: A list showing how much different court filings or services cost.
Example: The clerk provided the fee schedule listing the costs for filing a custody modification.

FEES
Definition: Payments required for court filings, services, or representation; in family law, fees include filing fees, service fees, or attorney's fees.
Explanation: Money paid to the court or professionals for their work or services.

Example: The mother asked the court to order the father to pay her attorney's fees after the custody trial.

FELDMAN DISCLOSURE SANCTIONS
Definition: Sanctions associated with In re Marriage of Feldman for failing to make complete and timely financial disclosures or to update important financial information. The court may award attorney's fees and monetary sanctions even when the undisclosed transaction did not cause a direct financial loss.
Explanation: A spouse can be sanctioned for hiding or delaying important financial information during divorce.
Example: The court imposed Feldman sanctions after Husband failed to disclose several major business transactions until shortly before trial.
See also: CONTINUING DUTY OF DISCLOSURE; PRELIMINARY DECLARATION OF DISCLOSURE; FINAL DECLARATION OF DISCLOSURE.

FILE
Definition: To officially submit a legal document to the court clerk so it becomes part of the case record; in family law, parties file petitions, motions, responses, and financial disclosures.
Explanation: To hand in official papers to the court so they become part of the case.
Example: The father went to the courthouse to file his response to the divorce petition.

FILE A MOTION
Definition: To formally request that the court take a specific action or make a ruling on an issue; in family law, motions may ask for temporary custody, support, or a change in visitation.
Explanation: To submit a written request asking the judge to decide on something in the case.
Example: The mother decided to file a motion for temporary child support while the divorce was pending.

FILE AN APPEAL
Definition: To initiate appellate proceedings by submitting a notice of appeal and required documents to challenge a Trial Court's decision; in family law, appeals may concern custody, visitation, support, or property division.

Explanation: To officially ask a higher court to review and change a lower court's decision.
Example: The father decided to file an appeal after the trial court denied his relocation request.

FILE SUIT

Definition: To commence a lawsuit by filing a complaint or petition in court; in family law, filing suit may involve divorce, custody, child support, or protective orders.
Explanation: To start a case in court by submitting the first legal papers.
Example: The wife chose to file suit for divorce after years of separation.

FILING FEE

Definition: The charge imposed by the court when a party submits a petition, motion, or other document to open or proceed with a case; in family law, filing fees apply to divorce petitions, custody requests, or modifications.
Explanation: Money paid to the court when submitting documents to start or continue a case.
Example: The mother paid the filing fee when she submitted her petition to modify child support.

FINAL DECLARATION OF DISCLOSURE

Definition: The later financial disclosure required before trial or judgment in most California dissolutions, unless both parties validly waive it in writing where waiver is allowed. It updates income, expenses, assets, debts, and material facts so settlement or trial occurs with current information.
Explanation: Before the divorce is finished, each spouse usually gives the other a final, updated financial picture.
Example: The parties exchanged final declarations of disclosure before signing their property settlement.
See also: OMITTED ASSET OR DEBT; FELDMAN DISCLOSURE SANCTIONS; SCHEDULE OF ASSETS AND DEBTS (FL-142).

FINAL JUDGMENT

Definition: The court's conclusive judgment resolving all remaining claims and issues, subject to any available review or enforcement.
Explanation: The final decision of the court that ends the case.

Example: The divorce was complete after the final judgment was entered.
See also: STATEMENT OF DECISION; JUDGMENT.

FINAL RESTRAINING ORDER
Definition: A long term protective order issued by the court after a hearing, prohibiting contact or harassment by the restrained party; in family law, final restraining orders are often granted in domestic violence cases to ensure the safety of the victim and children.
Explanation: A permanent order that stops one person from contacting or harming another after a court hearing.
Example: The court issued a final restraining order preventing the father from contacting the mother due to domestic violence.
See also: DOMESTIC VIOLENCE RESTRAINING ORDER.

FINANCE
Definition: The management of money, property, and economic resources; in family law, finance relates to determining income, expenses, debts, and assets to decide child support, spousal support, and division of property.
Explanation: Money matters such as income, debts, and property that courts consider in family cases.
Example: The divorce judgment included detailed provisions concerning the parties' finances, assets, and debts.

FINANCIAL INFORMATION
Definition: Data regarding a party's income, expenses, debts, and assets, provided to the court to assess support obligations or property division; disclosure is required in most family law proceedings.
Explanation: A person's money details, including what they earn, spend, owe, and own.
Example: The mother submitted financial information to support her claim for increased child support.

FINDING
Definition: A determination of fact made by a judge based on the evidence presented in a case; in family law, findings may relate to parental fitness, child's best interests, or financial capacity.
Explanation: A fact the judge decides is true after looking at the evidence.

Example: The court made a finding that the father had failed to comply with visitation orders.

FINDINGS AND ORDER AFTER HEARING (FOAH)
Definition: The written order, often prepared on form FL-340 with attachments, that records the Family Court's rulings after a hearing. California Rule of Court 5.125 sets procedures for preparing, serving, objecting to, and submitting the proposed order.
Explanation: The FOAH is the written version of what the judge ordered at the hearing.
Example: After the custody hearing, Mother's attorney prepared the FOAH and served it for review before submitting it to the judge.
See also: REQUEST FOR ORDER (RFO); COURT ORDER.

FIREARMS RELINQUISHMENT ORDER
Definition: An order requiring a person subject to a qualifying protective order to surrender, sell, or store firearms and ammunition and file proof of compliance within the legal deadlines. Possessing, buying, or receiving firearms or ammunition while prohibited can lead to criminal and civil consequences.
Explanation: A restrained person must promptly give up firearms and ammunition and prove it to the court.
Example: The respondent surrendered two firearms to law enforcement and filed the receipts required by the DVRO.
See also: DOMESTIC VIOLENCE RESTRAINING ORDER; CLETS ENTRY.

FIRST APPEARANCE
Definition: A general phrase for the first time a party appears before the court in a case. Unlike criminal procedure, an ordinary California family law case does not necessarily have one standardized event formally called the "first appearance"; the first event may be a request for order hearing, status conference, case management conference, or another locally scheduled proceeding.
Explanation: It means the party's first court appearance, but the hearing's formal name and purpose depend on the case and local procedure.
Example: At the first appearance, the judge set deadlines for exchanging financial information.

FOR THE RECORD

Definition: A phrase used in court to indicate that a statement is being made for inclusion in the official transcript, ensuring clarity and accuracy in the case record.
Explanation: Words spoken in court to make sure something is officially noted.
Example: The attorney stated for the record that both parties had agreed to the visitation schedule.

FORENSIC EVALUATION

Definition: A professional assessment ordered by the court, often psychological, to inform custody or visitation decisions.
Explanation: An expert study ordered by the court to guide decisions.
Example: The judge ordered a forensic evaluation in the custody matter.

FORM INTERROGATORIES

Definition: Standardized sets of written questions created by law or court rule that one party may send to another to obtain information in discovery; in family law, form interrogatories cover issues like income, assets, custody, and support.
Explanation: Prewritten lists of questions used in court cases to gather important information.
Example: The mother answered form interrogatories about her income and child care expenses in the divorce case.
See also: DISCOVERY.

FOSTER CARE

Definition: A system in which children who cannot safely live with their parents are placed in the temporary care of state licensed families or facilities; family law courts oversee foster care placements, permanency plans, and reunification efforts.
Explanation: Temporary care for children provided by another family or facility when parents cannot care for them.
Example: The judge ordered that the neglected child be placed in foster care until the parents completed reunification services.

FOSTER FAMILY

Definition: A family licensed by the state to provide temporary care and supervision for children placed in foster care; in family law, foster families work with courts and agencies to ensure children's safety.

Explanation: A family approved to take care of children temporarily when their own parents cannot.
Example: The foster family provided a safe home while the child's parents completed substance abuse treatment.

FOSTER HOME
Definition: A private residence licensed by the state to house children placed in foster care, either short term or long term, under the supervision of foster parents.
Explanation: A licensed home where children in foster care live temporarily.
Example: The child was placed in a foster home until a permanent placement could be arranged.

FRAUD
Definition: A deliberate misrepresentation or concealment of material facts intended to deceive another party, causing harm; in family law, fraud may invalidate prenuptial agreements, property settlements, or claims of parentage.
Explanation: Lying or hiding important facts to trick someone in a legal case.
Example: The court set aside the divorce settlement after finding the husband committed fraud by concealing assets.

FREEDOM FROM PARENTAL CUSTODY AND CONTROL
Definition: A California court proceeding that ends a parent's custody and control of a child, often so an adoption may proceed without that parent's consent. Grounds can include abandonment, neglect, disability in limited settings, or certain convictions, and the child's best interests remain important.
Explanation: This case asks the court to end a parent's legal power over a child, usually before adoption.
Example: The stepparent adoption proceeded after the court granted the petition for freedom from the absent parent's custody and control.
See also: STEPPARENT ADOPTION.

FREQUENT AND CONTINUING CONTACT
Definition: California's policy favoring regular contact with both parents after separation when that contact is consistent with the child's health, safety, welfare, and best interests. The policy does not override domestic

violence findings, abuse concerns, or other safety limits.
Explanation: Children should usually have ongoing relationships with both parents, but safety comes first.
Example: The parenting plan provided frequent contact with both parents while requiring supervised visits until the safety concerns were addressed.
See also: BEST INTERESTS OF THE CHILD; PARENTING TIME.

FRINGE BENEFITS
Definition: Non wage compensation provided by an employer, such as health insurance, retirement contributions, or company cars; in family law, fringe benefits are considered when calculating income for child or spousal support.
Explanation: Job benefits other than salary, like insurance or retirement, counted in support cases.
Example: The judge included the father's fringe benefits in calculating his child support obligation.

FROZEN BENEFIT RULE - MILITARY RETIRED PAY
Definition: A federal rule for dividing military retired pay in many divorces entered while the service member is still serving. The divisible benefit is generally based on the member's rank and years of service at divorce, with permitted cost of living adjustments, rather than later promotions or added service.
Explanation: The former spouse's share is usually based on the military career earned by the time of divorce, not future promotions after divorce.
Example: The military pension order used the member's rank and service credit as of the divorce date under the frozen benefit rule.
See also: MILITARY RETIRED PAY - 10/10 RULE.

FULL FAITH AND CREDIT FOR PROTECTIVE ORDERS
Definition: The federal rule requiring states, tribes, and territories to enforce qualifying protection orders issued by another jurisdiction as if the order were their own. The issuing court must have jurisdiction and the restrained person must have received notice and an opportunity to be heard, subject to emergency order rules.
Explanation: A valid restraining order usually follows the protected person across state lines.
Example: California law enforcement enforced the valid Arizona protection order after confirming its terms.

See also: PROTECTION ORDER; DOMESTIC VIOLENCE RESTRAINING ORDER; PARENTAL KIDNAPPING PREVENTION ACT (PKPA).

FULL TIME
Definition: Employment status where an individual works the standard number of hours defined by law or employer policy, typically 35–40 hours per week; in family law, full time work affects support obligations and parenting schedules.
Explanation: A regular work schedule of about 40 hours a week.
Example: The court considered the father's full time employment when setting the child support amount.

GARNISH
Definition: To require a third party, most commonly an employer, to withhold money owed to a judgment debtor and apply it to a legal obligation. Wages may be garnished; money in a bank account is ordinarily reached by a levy rather than described as garnishing the asset itself.
Explanation: A court order may require an employer to withhold part of a paycheck to pay support or another judgment.
Example: The mother requested the court to garnish the father's wages for overdue child support.

GARNISHMENT
Definition: The legal process of collecting money from a person's wages or bank account by court order to satisfy debts; in family law, wage garnishment is a common enforcement tool for support obligations.
Explanation: A process where the court takes money from wages or accounts to pay what is owed.
Example: The court ordered garnishment of the father's paycheck until child support arrears were paid.
See also: ARREARAGE (ARREARS); EXECUTION AGAINST WAGES; WAGE GARNISHMENT

GAVRON WARNING
Definition: A notice, based on In re Marriage of Gavron, that a supported spouse is expected to make reasonable efforts to become self supporting within a reasonable time. The warning does not automatically reduce support, but it may matter later if the supported spouse makes

inadequate efforts without good reason.
Explanation: The court warns the supported spouse to work toward financial independence when reasonably able.
Example: The judgment included a Gavron warning telling Wife to make reasonable efforts to obtain suitable employment.
See also: SPOUSAL SUPPORT; WORK SEARCH ORDER; VOCATIONAL EVALUATION; MORRISON RULE.

GENETIC MARKERS (DNA)
Definition: Specific sequences in a person's DNA used to establish biological relationships; in family law, genetic marker testing is a primary method for determining paternity and parentage.
Explanation: Pieces of DNA used in tests to prove if someone is a child's biological parent.
Example: The court relied on genetic markers from DNA testing to establish the father's paternity.

GESTATIONAL CARRIER AGREEMENT
Definition: A written assisted reproduction agreement in which a person agrees to carry a child conceived from an embryo not created with that carrier's egg for intended parent or parents. California law requires detailed terms, independent attorneys, proper signing before the medical procedure, and other safeguards.
Explanation: It is the formal contract used for a gestational surrogacy arrangement, and California requires careful legal steps before treatment begins.
Example: The intended parents and carrier each had separate lawyers and signed the agreement before embryo transfer.
See also: INTENDED PARENT; JOHNSON V. CALVERT INTENT TEST.

GILLMORE ELECTION
Definition: A right from In re Marriage of Gillmore that may allow the nonemployee spouse to receive the community share of a matured pension when the employee spouse is eligible to retire but chooses to keep working. The employee generally cannot defeat the other spouse's present interest merely by delaying retirement.
Explanation: When a pension is ready to pay, one spouse may not be able to postpone the other spouse's share by refusing to retire.
Example: Husband remained employed after becoming eligible to retire,

so Wife requested payments based on her Gillmore rights.
See also: DEFINED BENEFIT PLAN.

GOOD FAITH
Definition: Honest intention to act fairly, without deception or intent to defraud; in family law, good faith is required in disclosure of assets, negotiation of settlements, and compliance with court orders.
Explanation: Acting honestly and fairly in legal matters.
Example: The wife negotiated the property settlement in good faith, fully disclosing her assets.

GRANDPARENT CUSTODY PETITION
Definition: A legal request filed by grandparents asking the court to grant them custody of a grandchild, usually due to parental unfitness or absence.
Explanation: When grandparents ask the court to give them custody of their grandchild.
Example: The grandparents filed a custody petition after the parents were found unfit due to substance abuse.

GRANDPARENT VISITATION ORDER
Definition: A court order granting a grandparent visitation under a statute that permits the request. In California, the grandparent generally must show a preexisting relationship that has created a bond so that visitation is in the child's best interests, and the court must balance that interest against the parents' right to make decisions concerning the child; statutory standing limits also apply.
Explanation: A grandparent does not receive visitation merely by showing it would be beneficial; the statutory requirements and parental rights must also be satisfied.
Example: The court issued a grandparent visitation order to preserve the child's bond with grandparents.
See also: VISITATION RIGHTS.

GRANT A MOTION
Definition: A court's approval of a request made by a party through a formal motion; in family law, judges may grant motions for temporary custody, child support, or protective orders.
Explanation: When the judge agrees to a request made in writing.
Example: The judge decided to grant a motion for temporary child

support.

GROSS WAGES
Definition: Total earnings received by an employee before any taxes or deductions are taken out; in family law, gross wages are used to calculate support obligations.
Explanation: All the money someone earns before taxes or deductions.
Example: The judge used the father's gross wages to determine his monthly child support obligation.
See also: NET DISPOSABLE INCOME.

GROUNDS FOR DIVORCE
Definition: Legally recognized reasons permitting dissolution of marriage, including irreconcilable differences under California's no fault divorce law.
Explanation: The legal reasons why a marriage can be ended.
Example: The petition listed irreconcilable differences as grounds for divorce.

GUARDIAN
Definition: A person appointed by the court with legal authority to care for and make decisions on behalf of another person, usually a minor child or an incapacitated adult; in family law, a guardian may have authority over the child's person (care, custody, and upbringing) or estate (management of property and finances).
Explanation: Someone chosen by the court to take care of a child or their property when the parents cannot.
Example: The court appointed the aunt as guardian of the child after both parents were found unfit.
See also: GUARDIAN OF THE PERSON; GUARDIAN OF THE ESTATE; GUARDIAN AD LITEM.

GUARDIAN AD LITEM
Definition: A person appointed to protect the interests of a minor or an adult who lacks legal capacity during litigation. In California civil and family cases, a guardian ad litem acts for the party in the lawsuit but is not automatically the child's attorney, custody evaluator, or minor's counsel.
Explanation: The guardian ad litem makes litigation decisions for a party who cannot legally act alone in the case.

Example: The court appointed a guardian ad litem to act for the minor in the related civil proceeding.
See also: GUARDIAN.

GUARDIAN OF THE ESTATE
Definition: A person appointed by the court to manage and protect the financial assets, property, and legal affairs of a minor or incapacitated person, without necessarily having authority over personal care or custody.
Explanation: Someone chosen by the court to take care only of a child's money and property.
Example: The grandmother was appointed guardian of the estate to manage the child's inheritance until adulthood.
See also: GUARDIAN.

GUARDIAN OF THE ESTATE AND PERSON
Definition: A person appointed by the court with combined authority to care for both the personal needs (custody, education, medical decisions) and the financial matters (property, inheritance) of a minor or incapacitated person.
Explanation: Someone chosen by the court to care for both the child and the child's property.
Example: The court named the uncle guardian of the estate and person after both parents passed away.

GUARDIAN OF THE PERSON
Definition: A person appointed by the court with authority over the daily care, custody, education, and medical decisions of a minor or incapacitated person, but without control of financial assets unless specifically granted.
Explanation: Someone chosen by the court to care for a child's personal needs but not their money or property.
Example: The mother's sister was appointed guardian of the person to make medical and educational decisions for the child.
See also: GUARDIAN.

GUIDELINES
Definition: Rules or standards, often established by statute or court policy, that provide a framework for decision making; in family law, guidelines commonly refer to child support guidelines, which use income,

custody time, and other factors to calculate support obligations.
Explanation: Rules the court uses to help decide things like how much child support should be paid.
Example: The judge applied the state's child support guidelines to set the father's monthly payment.

HABITUAL RESIDENCE
Definition: The country or state where a child normally lives, often used in international custody disputes.
Explanation: The place where a child usually lives.
Example: The court considered the child's habitual residence in the Hague Convention case.
See also: HAGUE PETITION (INTERNATIONAL ABDUCTION).

HAGUE GRAVE RISK EXCEPTION
Definition: A narrow defense under Article 13(b) of the Hague Child Abduction Convention. A court may decline to return a wrongfully removed or retained child if clear and convincing evidence shows that return would expose the child to a grave risk of physical or psychological harm or an intolerable situation.
Explanation: A child may stay instead of being returned to another country only when the proven risk is very serious, not merely because one home seems better.
Example: The court examined whether protective measures could reduce the claimed grave risk before deciding the return petition.
See also: HAGUE PETITION (INTERNATIONAL ABDUCTION).

HAGUE PETITION (INTERNATIONAL ABDUCTION)
Definition: A legal request filed under the Hague Convention to secure the return of a child wrongfully removed or retained across international borders.
Explanation: A process to bring back a child taken illegally to another country.
Example: The father filed a Hague petition after the mother took the child abroad without consent.
See also: WRONGFUL REMOVAL/RETENTION; HABITUAL RESIDENCE; HAGUE GRAVE RISK EXCEPTION.

HAINES PRESUMPTION
Definition: A presumption of undue influence that may arise when one

spouse gains an unfair advantage from an interspousal transaction. Under In re Marriage of Haines and the spouses' fiduciary duties, the advantaged spouse may have to prove that the transaction was freely and knowingly made.
Explanation: When a deal between spouses strongly favors one spouse, that spouse may have to prove the deal was fair and voluntary.
Example: Husband had to rebut the Haines presumption after Wife signed away her interest in the home without advice or a clear explanation.
See also: TRANSMUTATION / MACDONALD EXPRESS DECLARATION RULE; SPOUSAL FIDUCIARY DUTY / SECTION 1101 REMEDIES.

HARASSMENT
Definition: Unwanted conduct that causes alarm or distress, often the basis for restraining orders in family cases.
Explanation: When someone repeatedly bothers or threatens another person.
Example: She filed for a restraining order based on harassment.
See also: CYBER HARASSMENT.

HARDSHIP DEDUCTION
Definition: A limited deduction from net disposable income for specified severe financial hardships when calculating child support. Qualifying hardships can include extraordinary health expenses, uninsured catastrophic losses, or minimum living expenses of certain children in the parent's home. The court decides the amount and duration.
Explanation: The support calculation may allow a temporary deduction for certain serious expenses, but not for every debt or financial problem.
Example: The court allowed a six month hardship deduction for the parent's uninsured medical expenses after major surgery.
See also: CHILD SUPPORT GUIDELINES DEVIATION; LOW INCOME ADJUSTMENT.

HEALTH INSURANCE
Definition: A contract that provides coverage for medical care and treatment; in family law, courts may require one or both parents to maintain health insurance for their children as part of a support order.
Explanation: Medical coverage that a parent may be required to provide

for their child.
Example: The divorce decree required the father to maintain health insurance for the children through his employer.

HEAR A CASE
Definition: The act of a court or judge reviewing arguments, evidence, and testimony to make a decision on legal issues; in family law, judges hear cases involving custody, visitation, support, and domestic violence.
Explanation: When the judge listens to both sides and decides the outcome of a legal dispute.
Example: The judge heard the custody case, considered testimony and exhibits, and issued a written ruling.

HEARING
Definition: A formal court session where parties present arguments, evidence, and testimony on specific issues; in family law, hearings resolve matters such as temporary custody, child support, or restraining orders.
Explanation: A court meeting where evidence is presented and the judge makes a decision.
Example: At the custody hearing, both parents testified about their ability to care for the child.

HEARING OFFICER
Definition: A judicial officer or quasi-judicial official who conducts hearings, takes evidence, and makes recommendations or rulings; in family law, hearing officers may handle support calculations or preliminary matters under court supervision.
Explanation: A court official, not always a judge, who runs hearings and makes recommendations or decisions.
Example: The child support issue was decided by a hearing officer appointed by the court.

HEARSAY
Definition: An out of court statement offered in court to prove the truth of the matter asserted, generally inadmissible unless an exception applies; in family law, hearsay may arise in testimony about what a child allegedly said.
Explanation: Hearsay is an out of court statement offered to prove what the statement asserts. It is not limited to "secondhand" information and may include the testifying witness's own earlier statement.

Example: The court sustained a hearsay objection when the witness repeated the absent neighbor's statement to prove that the alleged event occurred and no exception applied.
See also: EVIDENCE CODE SECTION 1200 - HEARSAY; HEARSAY EVIDENCE; BUSINESS RECORDS EXCEPTION.

HEARSAY EVIDENCE
Definition: Evidence consisting of hearsay statements, which are generally excluded unless they fit within statutory or common law exceptions, such as business records or excited utterances.
Explanation: Evidence based on repeating what someone else said, not direct knowledge.
Example: The father's lawyer objected to hearsay evidence when the mother tried to introduce a letter from a neighbor.
See also: HEARSAY.

HEREBY
Definition: A formal legal term used in documents to indicate that an action is being taken by virtue of the statement itself; it gives immediate effect to what follows.
Explanation: A formal word in legal documents meaning "by this statement."
Example: The order stated, "The court hereby grants custody of the minor child to the mother."

HIGH EARNER EXCEPTION
Definition: A ground for departing from guideline child support when the support obligor has extraordinarily high income and the guideline amount would exceed the child's needs. The exception is narrow, and the child's right to share in the parent's standard of living remains important.
Explanation: A very high earner may seek less than the formula amount only by proving that the formula would exceed the child's reasonable needs.
Example: The athlete presented evidence of the child's actual needs, but the court also considered the child's right to share in the athlete's high standard of living.
See also: CHILD SUPPORT GUIDELINES DEVIATION.

HOLIDAY
Definition: A recognized day of rest or celebration, often specified in

custody and visitation schedules to determine which parent will spend time with the child on that date.
Explanation: A special day like Christmas or Thanksgiving, often divided between parents in custody orders.
Example: The parenting plan alternated custody on each holiday.

HOME ADDRESS

Definition: The residential address where a party or child lives, often required for jurisdiction, service of process, or enforcement of custody orders; courts may restrict disclosure of home addresses in cases involving safety concerns.
Explanation: The place where someone or a child lives for legal purposes.
Example: The custody order required each parent to keep the court updated with their current home address.
See also: ADDRESS CONFIDENTIALITY PROGRAM.

HOME STATE

Definition: Under the UCCJEA, the state in which a child lived with a parent or person acting as a parent for at least six consecutive months immediately before commencement of the custody proceeding. For a child younger than six months, it is the state where the child lived from birth with such a person; temporary absences are included.
Explanation: It is usually the state where the child lived during the six months immediately before the first custody filing, with special rules for infants and temporary absences.
Example: California was the child's home state because the child lived here with a parent for the six consecutive months immediately before the case began.
See also: UNIFORM CHILD CUSTODY JURISDICTION AND ENFORCEMENT ACT (UCCJEA); SIGNIFICANT CONNECTION JURISDICTION - UCCJEA.

HOME STUDY REPORT (ADOPTION)

Definition: An evaluation prepared by a social worker or agency assessing the suitability of prospective adoptive parents' home and background.
Explanation: A report checking if adoptive parents' home is suitable for adoption.
Example: The agency submitted a home study report before the

adoption was approved.
See: ADOPTION HOME STUDY

HOSTILE WITNESS
Definition: A witness who demonstrates bias, resistance, or antagonism toward the party who called them to testify; in family law, a hostile witness may be cross examined by the calling party as if by the opposing side, using leading questions.
Explanation: A witness who refuses to cooperate or shows bias, so the lawyer can question them more strictly.
Example: The mother was declared a hostile witness when she resisted answering questions about the parenting schedule.

HOUSING
Definition: Residential arrangements or accommodations where a parent or child lives; in family law, housing conditions are considered when determining custody, visitation, and the child's best interests.
Explanation: The living place or conditions where a parent or child resides.
Example: The judge reviewed the father's housing situation before granting overnight visitation.

HUG/NELSON STOCK OPTION FORMULAS
Definition: Two time rule approaches used to characterize employee stock options earned partly during marriage. The Hug approach is commonly used when the grant mainly rewards past services, while Nelson is commonly used when the grant mainly encourages future service or retention. The grant's actual purpose controls.
Explanation: Different formulas may divide stock options depending on whether they reward past work or future work.
Example: The court used a Nelson type formula after the grant documents showed that the options were mainly intended to keep the employee working through vesting.

ICWA PLACEMENT PREFERENCES
Definition: Federal and California preferences for placing an Indian child with extended family, members of the child's tribe, other Indian families, or other preferred placements, depending on the type of case. A court may depart from the preferences only under the governing good cause standards.

Explanation: When an Indian child needs placement, the law favors family and tribal connections.
Example: The agency first searched for relatives and tribal homes before proposing a non Indian foster placement.
See also: INDIAN CHILD WELFARE ACT (ICWA).

IMPEACH A WITNESS
Definition: The process of challenging the credibility, truthfulness, or reliability of a witness's testimony by showing inconsistencies, bias, or prior contradictory statements; in family law, this may occur when a witness gives conflicting accounts about custody or financial matters.
Explanation: To show that a witness is not telling the truth or cannot be trusted.
Example: The father's attorney moved to impeach a witness by introducing her earlier inconsistent statement about visitation.

IMPEACHMENT
Definition: The broader legal process of discrediting evidence or testimony by proving it unreliable, inconsistent, or biased; in family law, impeachment helps ensure the court bases decisions on trustworthy testimony.
Explanation: The act of proving that testimony or evidence is not reliable.
Example: The mother's lawyer used impeachment when the father contradicted his financial disclosure.

IMPLIED CONTRACT BETWEEN COHABITANTS
Definition: An unwritten agreement inferred from the conduct and circumstances of unmarried partners, showing an understanding to share property, earnings, or support. Courts may enforce implied contracts under Marvin v. Marvin.
Explanation: An agreement the court assumes exists between partners because of how they lived and acted, even if not written down.
Example: The court found an implied contract between the partners to share property because they had pooled their income for 15 years.

IMPOSE
Definition: To order or enforce an obligation, penalty, or requirement by authority of the court; in family law, a court may impose child support, sanctions for contempt, or restrictions on visitation.

Explanation: When the judge orders something that must be followed.
Example: The judge decided to impose a fine for the father's repeated failure to comply with visitation orders.

IMPROPER MOTIVES

Definition: Reasons for acting that are dishonest, unfair, or intended to harm, rather than to serve a legitimate legal purpose; in family law, improper motives may appear in custody disputes where one parent seeks to limit access out of spite.
Explanation: Acting for the wrong reasons, not for fairness or the child's best interests.
Example: The court found that the mother's objection to visitation was based on improper motives of revenge.

IMPUTED INCOME (SUPPORT CASES)

Definition: Income assigned by the court to a parent based on earning capacity rather than actual earnings, used to calculate child or spousal support.
Explanation: Income the court assumes a parent could earn, used for support calculations.
Example: The court used imputed income to calculate support after the father quit his job.
See also: VOCATIONAL EVALUATION; WORK SEARCH ORDER.

IN CAMERA INTERVIEW OF CHILD

Definition: A method by which a judge receives a child's views outside the parents' presence, subject to California law and Rule 5.250 concerning child participation, a suitable setting, protection from pressure or harm, and creation of an appropriate record.
Explanation: The judge may hear from the child in a protected setting, but the court must follow the rules governing how the child participates and how the information is recorded.
Example: The judge held an in camera interview of the child to consider her wishes in the custody case.
See also: MINOR'S COUNSEL.

IN LOCO PARENTIS DOCTRINE

Definition: A general doctrine describing a person who has assumed parental functions in place of a parent. In California, acting in loco parentis does not by itself necessarily create legal parentage or custody

rights; the facts may instead be relevant to presumed parentage, guardianship, de facto parent status, or another statutory doctrine.
Explanation: A person's parental role may matter, but a recognized legal basis is still required for custody, visitation, or parentage orders.
Example: The longtime caregiver sought presumed parent status and, alternatively, guardianship rather than relying only on the label in loco parentis.

INADMISSIBLE
Definition: Evidence that cannot be considered by the court because it does not meet the rules of evidence, such as relevance, reliability, or compliance with procedure; in family law, inadmissible evidence may include hearsay or improperly obtained documents.
Explanation: Evidence the judge is not allowed to consider in making a decision.
Example: The father's attorney objected, and the judge ruled the text messages were inadmissible.
See also: ADMISSIBILITY.

INCOME
Definition: Money earned or received from any source, including wages, salaries, bonuses, investments, or benefits; in family law, income is the primary factor used to calculate child support and spousal support.
Explanation: All money a person earns or receives, which is used to decide support payments.
Example: The court reviewed income records to set child support.

INCOME AND EXPENSE DECLARATION
Definition: A Judicial Council form disclosing a party's income, expenses, assets, debts, and other financial information in a family law case.
Explanation: A form that shows your income and expenses to the court.
Example: He filed an income and expense declaration in the support case.

INCOME WITHHOLDING ORDER
Definition: A court order directing an employer to deduct child or spousal support from a paycheck.
Explanation: An order that makes the employer take support money from a paycheck.

Example: The employer received an income withholding order for child support.
See also: ASSIGNMENT ORDER (EARNINGS ASSIGNMENT); WAGE ASSIGNMENT (EARNINGS ASSIGNMENT ORDER); STATE DISBURSEMENT UNIT (SDU).

INCONVENIENT FORUM - UCCJEA
Definition: A rule allowing a court with custody jurisdiction to decline the case because another state is the more appropriate forum. The court considers domestic violence, how long the child lived elsewhere, distance, finances, party agreement, location of evidence, court speed, and each court's familiarity with the facts.
Explanation: A court may send the custody case to another state that can handle it more safely and effectively.
Example: California stayed the case after finding that most witnesses, records, and the child were in Oregon and that Oregon was the better forum.
See also: UNJUSTIFIABLE CONDUCT - UCCJEA.

INCULPATORY STATEMENT
Definition: A statement made by a person that tends to show their own involvement in wrongdoing or liability; in family law, an inculpatory statement might arise in contempt proceedings or admissions of violating custody or support orders.
Explanation: A statement where someone admits or suggests they did something wrong.
Example: The father's inculpatory statement that he "knew he wasn't supposed to take the child" was used in the contempt hearing.

INCUR
Definition: To become liable for or bring upon oneself a debt, expense, or obligation; in family law, a parent may incur expenses for child care, medical care, or educational costs.
Explanation: To take on or become responsible for a cost or obligation.
Example: The mother did not want to incur additional daycare expenses without the father's contribution.

INDEPENDENT ADOPTION AGENCY
Definition: A licensed private agency that arranges adoptions outside of the state or public foster care system.

Explanation: A private agency that handles adoptions outside the government system.
Example: They worked with an independent adoption agency to adopt a child from another state.
See also: AGENCY ADOPTION.

INDIAN CHILD WELFARE ACT (ICWA)
Definition: Federal and California laws governing child custody proceedings involving an Indian child. ICWA can require inquiry, notice to tribes, tribal participation, active efforts, special proof, qualified expert testimony, and placement preferences. Tribal citizenship and eligibility are decided by the tribe, not by appearance or family belief alone.
Explanation: ICWA protects an Indian child's family and tribal ties and gives the tribe an important role in the case.
Example: The court delayed the guardianship hearing until the tribe received proper notice and could decide whether to intervene.
See also: ACTIVE EFFORTS - ICWA; ICWA PLACEMENT PREFERENCES; QUALIFIED EXPERT WITNESS - ICWA; REASON TO KNOW AN INDIAN CHILD IS INVOLVED.

INDIGENCE
Definition: Financial inability to pay court fees, litigation expenses, or counsel. In a California family law case, indigence may support a fee waiver, but it does not ordinarily create a right to a court appointed lawyer in a routine divorce or custody dispute.
Explanation: A person who cannot afford court fees may ask for a waiver; free counsel is available only when another law provides it.
Example: The parent applied for a fee waiver because income and available resources were insufficient to pay the filing fee.

INDIGENCE DETERMINATION
Definition: A determination that a person meets the financial criteria for a particular benefit or protection, such as waiver of court fees. The determination is purpose specific and does not automatically establish eligibility for appointed counsel.
Explanation: The judge's decision about whether someone is too poor to pay court costs.
Example: After reviewing the fee waiver application, the court waived the filing fees but did not appoint counsel.

INDIGENCY
Definition: The legally relevant condition of being unable to afford specified court costs or representation. In California civil and family matters, indigency commonly relates to fee waivers; appointment of counsel requires a separate constitutional or statutory basis.
Explanation: The term concerns financial inability, but the available relief depends on the proceeding.
Example: The party asserted indigency in support of a request to waive court fees.

INDIGENT
Definition: Unable to afford specified legal costs. An indigent party may qualify for a fee waiver and may receive appointed counsel only in a proceeding where the law independently provides that right.
Explanation: Financial hardship may waive fees, but it does not automatically provide a free lawyer in every family law case.
Example: The court appointed an attorney for the indigent father in the parental rights termination case.

INHERITANCE
Definition: Property received from a deceased person's estate. In California, an inheritance received by one spouse is generally that spouse's separate property. Depositing or using the inheritance with community funds may create tracing, reimbursement, title, or transmutation issues, but commingling alone does not automatically make the inheritance community property.
Explanation: Assets passed down to a person when someone dies.
Example: The inheritance remained separate because records traced the funds and no valid transmutation changed its character.
See also: COMMINGLING.

INITIAL APPEARANCE
Definition: A general phrase for a party's first appearance before a court. Ordinary California family law procedure does not require one uniform hearing formally called an "initial appearance"; the first scheduled event depends on the type of request and local practice.
Explanation: It means the first time the party appears, but the event may be a custody hearing, support hearing, status conference, or another proceeding.
Example: At the initial appearance, the judge scheduled mediation for

the custody dispute.

INJUNCTION

Definition: A court order directing a party to do or refrain from doing specific acts; in family law, injunctions may prevent harassment, asset transfers, or relocation of children.
Explanation: A judge's order telling someone to stop or start doing something specific.
Example: The court issued an injunction preventing the father from selling community property during the divorce.

INJURED SPOUSE CLAIM

Definition: A request made to the IRS by a spouse who files a joint tax return to protect their portion of a refund from being used to pay the other spouse's debts, such as overdue child support.
Explanation: A tax request that protects one spouse's refund money from being taken for the other spouse's debts.
Example: The wife filed an injured spouse claim to recover her share of the tax refund used to pay the husband's child support arrears.

INSTALLMENT

Definition: A partial payment of a total debt or obligation, made in scheduled portions over time; in family law, child support or spousal support may be ordered to be paid in monthly installments.
Explanation: Paying part of what is owed in regular scheduled payments.
Example: The father was ordered to pay child support in monthly installments of $500.

INSURANCE

Definition: A contractual arrangement in which an insurer agrees to provide financial protection against specified risks in exchange for premiums; in family law, parents may be required to maintain health, dental, or life insurance for their children.
Explanation: Coverage that pays for losses or medical needs, sometimes ordered for children in custody cases.
Example: The divorce decree required the father to maintain health insurance for the child until age 18.

INTACT
Definition: In family law, used to describe a family structure in which both parents live together with their children; also used to refer to property or documents that remain whole and unchanged.
Explanation: Complete and not broken apart, often used for families or property.
Example: The judge noted that the child had grown up in an intact family until the divorce proceedings began.

INTENDED PARENT
Definition: A person who intends to be legally bound as a child's parent through assisted reproduction, including a qualifying gestational carrier arrangement. Intent must be shown in the manner required by California law and may be established through a valid agreement and parentage order.
Explanation: The intended parent is the person who planned and legally agreed to become the child's parent through assisted reproduction.
Example: The prebirth parentage order named both spouses as intended parents under their valid gestational carrier agreement.
See also: DONOR NOT A PARENT; GESTATIONAL CARRIER AGREEMENT.

INTENT
Definition: The state of mind with which a person acts, showing purpose, design, or aim; in family law, intent may be relevant in proving fraud, parental alienation, or the willful violation of court orders.
Explanation: The reason or purpose behind a person's actions.
Example: The court found that the father's intent in denying visitation was to alienate the child from the mother.

INTEREST ON SUPPORT ARREARS
Definition: Interest that accrues on unpaid child or spousal support installments after they become due. California generally charges simple interest at 10 percent per year on unpaid support judgments, although federal protections such as the SCRA may lower the rate for qualifying pre service debt.
Explanation: Late support usually grows because interest is added to the unpaid balance.
Example: Although Father later paid the missed principal, he still owed the interest that had accrued on each overdue installment.

See also: ARREARAGE (ARREARS); SUPPORT RETROACTIVITY.

INTERIM
Definition: Temporary in nature, often used to describe orders or measures issued to remain in effect until a final hearing; in family law, interim custody or support orders are common while the case is pending.
Explanation: A temporary order until the court makes a final decision.
Example: The judge issued an interim order granting the mother primary custody until trial.

INTERROGATORY
Definition: A set of written questions formally submitted by one party to another as part of discovery, requiring written answers under oath; in family law, interrogatories are often used to gather information about income, assets, and parenting ability.
Explanation: Written questions that one side must answer in writing under oath before trial.
Example: The mother served an interrogatory asking the father about his employment history and income.

INTRODUCTION
Definition: The opening section of a legal document that explains its purpose, scope, or background; in family law, introductions may appear in agreements, parenting plans, or reports to outline the issues being addressed.
Explanation: The beginning part of a legal paper that explains what it is about.
Example: The introduction of the parenting plan stated that the parties wished to prioritize the child's best interests.

INVESTMENT
Definition: Money or other resources committed to an asset or venture with an expectation of income or appreciation. In a dissolution, an investment must be disclosed and may be community property, separate property, or a mixture of both depending on acquisition, funding, title, tracing, and agreements.
Explanation: Investments must be disclosed, but only the community portion is generally divided in a California divorce.
Example: The court divided the community portion of the investment account and confirmed the traceable premarital portion as separate

property.

IRRECONCILABLE DIFFERENCES

Definition: A common legal ground for divorce meaning the spouses cannot get along and the marriage cannot be saved.

Explanation: When a marriage can't be fixed because the couple can't get along.

Example: The petition for divorce was based on irreconcilable differences.

IRRELEVANT

Definition: Evidence, statements, or arguments that do not relate to the issues being decided in a case and therefore have no probative value; in family law, irrelevant matters are excluded to keep the focus on custody, support, or property questions that affect the child's best interests or equitable division.

Explanation: Information that does not matter to the legal question the judge must decide.

Example: The judge ruled that details about the father's teenage years were irrelevant to the custody decision.

ISSUE

Definition: A disputed question of fact or law that the court must resolve; in family law, issues may include custody, visitation, child support, spousal support, domestic violence, or property division.

Explanation: A legal question or conflict that the judge must decide.

Example: The main issue in the divorce was whether joint custody would serve the child's best interests.

JACKSON/TRAINOTTI CREDITS

Definition: A possible equitable credit against support arrears when the paying parent directly housed and supported the child during a period covered by an existing order. The credit is fact specific and treats the obligation as satisfied in whole or part; it is not a general power to erase or retroactively modify accrued support.

Explanation: A parent may receive credit for actually supporting the child during a time the child lived with that parent, but the result is not automatic.

Example: The court credited documented months when the child lived full time with Father and he paid all daily expenses with Mother's

agreement.
See also: SUPPORT RETROACTIVITY; ARREARAGE (ARREARS).

JEFFRIES CREDITS

Definition: A reimbursement credit recognized in California divorce cases when one spouse pays community obligations with separate funds under circumstances not covered by Epstein, often involving fairness considerations.
Explanation: A spouse may be reimbursed for paying joint debts with their own money, in situations where Epstein credits don't directly apply.
Example: The court awarded Jeffries credits when the wife used her separate inheritance to pay off community credit card debt.
See also: EPSTEIN CREDITS.

JOHNSON V. CALVERT INTENT TEST

Definition: A parentage principle from Johnson v. Calvert used in assisted reproduction cases when genetic and birth claims point to different people. The court may identify the legal parent by determining who intended to bring about the child's birth and raise the child as a parent, subject to current statutes and agreements.
Explanation: In some assisted reproduction disputes, the planned and agreed parental intent helps decide legal parentage.
Example: The intended mother was declared the legal parent because the valid arrangement showed that she and her spouse initiated the pregnancy to raise the child.
See also: GESTATIONAL CARRIER AGREEMENT.

JOINDER (INCLUDING RETIREMENT PLAN JOINDER)

Definition: The procedure for adding a person or entity whose rights or control are necessary for the Family Court to decide or enforce an issue. A retirement plan may need to be joined before the court can divide benefits or bind the plan, although federal and plan specific rules vary.
Explanation: A needed third party, such as a pension plan, is formally added to the family law case.
Example: The court ordered joinder of the pension plan before entering the order dividing the employee's benefits.
See also: DOMESTIC RELATIONS ORDER (DRO).

JOINT CUSTODY

Definition: A custody arrangement where both parents share legal

and/or physical custody of a child.
Explanation: When both parents share responsibility for the child.
Example: The court awarded joint custody to both parents.
See also: JOINT LEGAL CUSTODY; JOINT PHYSICAL CUSTODY.

JOINT LEGAL CUSTODY

Definition: Both parents share the right to make important decisions about the child's welfare, education, and health.
Explanation: Both parents have a say in major decisions for the child.
Example: They share joint legal custody, so both must agree on schooling.
See also: LEGAL CUSTODY; JOINT CUSTODY.

JOINT PHYSICAL CUSTODY

Definition: A custody arrangement in which each parent has significant periods of physical custody, promoting frequent and continuing contact with the child.
Explanation: The child lives part time with each parent.
Example: The order granted joint physical custody, with the child spending alternating weeks in each parent's home.
See also: JOINT CUSTODY; WEEK ON/WEEK OFF SCHEDULE; PARENTING TIME.

JUDGE

Definition: A public official authorized to preside over court proceedings, rule on evidence and procedure, interpret and apply law, make factual findings, and enter orders or judgments. In family law, the governing standard depends on the issue; the child's best interests control custody questions, while statutes and other legal standards govern support, property, fees, and procedural matters.
Explanation: The person in charge of the courtroom who listens to both sides and makes the final decisions.
Example: The judge awarded joint legal custody but gave the mother primary physical custody of the children.

JUDGMENT

Definition: A court's final determination of the parties' rights and obligations concerning the claims decided in a case.
Explanation: The court's final decision in a case.
Example: The divorce judgment was entered last week.

See also: FINAL JUDGMENT; ENTRY OF JUDGMENT.

JUDICIAL CHALLENGE

Definition: A time limited peremptory challenge under Code of Civil Procedure § 170.6 to a California judge, commissioner, or referee based on a sworn statement that the judicial officer is prejudiced against the party or attorney. The challenger ordinarily does not have to prove actual bias, but strict timing and one challenge limits apply.
Explanation: A party may usually disqualify one assigned judicial officer without proving bias, but the challenge must be filed on time.
Example: Counsel filed a timely Section 170.6 challenge before the assigned judge ruled on any contested issue.

JUDICIAL CUSTODY DETERMINATION

Definition: A custody decision made by a judge after reviewing evidence and testimony, focusing on the best interests of the child.
Explanation: A judge's decision about who gets custody of the child.
Example: The judicial custody determination awarded sole custody to the father.

JUDICIAL OFFICER

Definition: A person authorized by law to exercise judicial functions, including judges, magistrates, commissioners, or referees; in family law, judicial officers preside over hearings, issue orders, and resolve disputes involving custody, support, and protection.
Explanation: An official, such as a judge or magistrate, who has the power to make legal decisions in court.
Example: The judicial officer presided over the child support hearing and entered an enforceable order.

JUDICIARY

Definition: The branch of government responsible for interpreting laws and administering justice through the court system; in family law, the judiciary includes Family Courts, judges, and administrative staff handling domestic cases.
Explanation: The court system, made up of judges and staff, that interprets and applies the law.
Example: The state judiciary established a specialized family division to handle divorce and custody cases.

JURISDICTION
Definition: The legal authority of a court to hear and decide a case, based on subject matter, geography, or the parties involved; in family law, jurisdiction is critical for divorce, custody, and adoption proceedings, often determined by where the child or parties reside.
Explanation: The court's legal power to hear a case and make decisions.
Example: The court lacked jurisdiction to modify custody because the child no longer lived in the state.

JUSTIFICATION
Definition: A legal defense or explanation showing that an action, otherwise unlawful, was reasonable or legally excusable under the circumstances; in family law, justification may be raised in contempt cases or when explaining missed visitation or support payments.
Explanation: A valid legal reason or excuse for doing something that might otherwise be considered wrong.
Example: The father offered justification for missing visitation by showing he was hospitalized at the time.

KELSEY S. FATHER
Definition: An unwed biological father who promptly comes forward, fully commits to parental responsibilities, and is prevented by others from obtaining ordinary presumed parent status. Under Adoption of Kelsey S., such a father may have constitutional protection against adoption without consent unless the court makes the required finding of unfitness.
Explanation: A committed biological father may gain strong parental protection when he acted promptly but was blocked from receiving the child into his home.
Example: The court examined whether Father paid pregnancy expenses, sought custody immediately, and consistently tried to assume full parental duties.

KINSHIP CARE
Definition: When relatives care for children who cannot live with their parents, often approved by the court.
Explanation: When family members take care of children instead of parents.
Example: The grandmother provided kinship care for the children.

KNOWINGLY

Definition: With full awareness and intent, acting with knowledge of the facts or consequences; in family law, knowingly may describe violations of custody orders, failure to pay support, or acts of domestic violence done with awareness of their illegality.

Explanation: Doing something on purpose, knowing what you are doing is against the rules or law.

Example: The father was found in contempt for knowingly refusing to return the child after visitation.

LAMUSGA FACTORS

Definition: Move away considerations from In re Marriage of LaMusga, including the distance of the move, the child's age and wishes, the existing parenting arrangement, the parents' relationship and communication, the reasons for the move, and whether a workable plan can preserve the child's relationship with both parents.

Explanation: The judge looks at the practical effect of a proposed move on the child and the child's relationships.

Example: The court focused on travel time, school schedules, the child's bond with Father, and Mother's willingness to support contact after the move.

See also: MOVE AWAY CASE.

LAW

Definition: The system of rules, statutes, and judicial decisions established by governing authorities and enforced through courts; in family law, statutes and case law regulate marriage, divorce, custody, support, and adoption.

Explanation: The set of rules created and enforced by government and courts.

Example: The lawyer argued that state law required child custody decisions to focus on the best interests of the child.

LAW CLERK

Definition: A trained legal assistant, often a recent law graduate, who supports judges by researching legal issues, drafting opinions, and reviewing case files; in family law, clerks help judges analyze statutes and case law on custody and support.

Explanation: A legal assistant who helps a judge by researching and drafting documents.

Example: The law clerk researched case law on relocation disputes for the family court judge.

LAW ENFORCEMENT AGENCY
Definition: A governmental body authorized to enforce laws, maintain public order, and protect individuals; in family law, law enforcement agencies may enforce protective orders, assist in child recovery, or ensure compliance with custody exchanges.
Explanation: A police or government agency that enforces laws and court orders.
Example: The mother contacted the law enforcement agency to enforce the restraining order after the father appeared at her home.

LAW LIBRARY
Definition: A specialized library containing legal texts, statutes, case law, and practice guides used by attorneys, judges, and the public; in family law, law libraries provide resources for legal research on divorce, custody, and support.
Explanation: A library with legal books and resources for research.
Example: The self represented parent used the law library to find cases about child support modification.

LAWFUL
Definition: Permitted or authorized by law; in family law, lawful actions include properly filed petitions, lawful custody, and lawful marriage.
Explanation: Something that is allowed by law.
Example: The court confirmed that the marriage was lawful under state law.

LAWSUIT
Definition: A legal proceeding brought before a court by one party against another seeking relief or enforcement of rights; in family law, lawsuits may involve divorce, custody, support, or annulment.
Explanation: A case started in court by filing legal papers asking for a ruling.
Example: The mother filed a lawsuit for divorce, seeking custody and child support.

LAWYER
Definition: A professional licensed to practice law, represent clients in

court, provide legal advice, and prepare legal documents; in family law, lawyers handle divorce, custody, support, adoption, and domestic violence matters.
Explanation: A person trained and licensed to represent and advise clients in court.
Example: The father hired a lawyer to represent him in the child custody case.

LEADING QUESTION
Definition: A question that suggests the desired answer. Leading questions are ordinarily permitted on cross examination and when examining an adverse or hostile witness, and may also be allowed on direct examination for preliminary, undisputed, or other proper purposes in the court's discretion.
Explanation: The question points toward an answer; whether it is allowed depends on who is being questioned and why.
Example: During cross examination, the attorney asked the witness a leading question: "Isn't it true you never saw the father at the child's school?"

LEGAL CUSTODY
Definition: The right to make important decisions about a child's life, including education, health care, and welfare.
Explanation: The power to decide about a child's schooling, health, and care.
Example: She was granted sole legal custody of her son.
See also: CHILD CUSTODY; LEGAL DECISION MAKING; JOINT LEGAL CUSTODY.

LEGAL DECISION MAKING
Definition: The authority to make major decisions concerning a child's health, education, religion, and welfare; in jurisdictions using this terminology, it replaces the older term legal custody.
Explanation: The term identifies who decides important matters for the child. California statutes generally use legal custody, while some other jurisdictions use legal decision making.
Example: The order awarded joint legal decision making, requiring both parents to participate in major educational and medical decisions.
See also: CUSTODY; LEGAL CUSTODY; PARENTING TIME.

LEGAL SEPARATION

Definition: A court order allowing a married couple to live apart while still legally married, often addressing custody and support.
Explanation: When a couple lives apart by court order but is not divorced.
Example: They obtained a legal separation instead of divorce.

LEHMAN PENSION ENHANCEMENT RULE

Definition: A retirement rule from In re Marriage of Lehman that may give the community a share of postseparation pension enhancements when those enhancements are part of the benefit earned from service during marriage. The result depends on the plan, the nature of the increase, and the division formula.
Explanation: Some later pension increases may be shared when they grow from service performed during the marriage.
Example: The former spouse's share included a plan enhancement tied to the employee's years of service, including the years served during marriage.
See also: DEFINED BENEFIT PLAN.

LIABILITY

Definition: A legal obligation or responsibility to act or to refrain from acting in a certain way, or to compensate for harm or debt; in family law, liability may include responsibility for child support, spousal support, or debts incurred during the marriage.
Explanation: A legal responsibility that requires someone to pay money or fulfill an obligation.
Example: The divorce decree established joint liability for the couple's credit card debts.

LIMITED SCOPE REPRESENTATION (FAMILY LAW)

Definition: When a lawyer represents a client for only part of a case, such as preparing documents or appearing at one hearing, instead of the entire case.
Explanation: When a lawyer helps with only some parts of a case, not the whole case.
Example: She hired a lawyer for limited scope representation to prepare her custody documents.

LITIGANT
Definition: A party directly involved in a lawsuit, either as a petitioner, respondent, plaintiff, or defendant; in family law, litigants include spouses, parents, or guardians engaged in disputes over custody, support, or divorce.
Explanation: A person who is part of a case in court.
Example: Both litigants presented evidence at the custody hearing.

LITIGATE
Definition: To bring a dispute before a court for resolution through the legal process; in family law, to litigate means to pursue contested issues such as custody, visitation, property division, or support through hearings and trials.
Explanation: To take a dispute to court so a judge can decide.
Example: The parents chose to litigate the custody dispute after mediation failed.

LITIGATION
Definition: The formal process of resolving legal disputes through pleadings, discovery, hearings, trial, and possible appellate review.
Explanation: Fighting a case in court.
Example: The custody case went into litigation.

LIVE SCAN
Definition: An electronic method of capturing fingerprints and transmitting them for a background check. Live Scan may be required in adoption, foster care, guardianship, and other proceedings involving child safety.
Explanation: Live Scan electronically submits fingerprints for a criminal history background check.
Example: The prospective adoptive parents completed Live Scan fingerprinting before the adoption hearing.

LOCAL CHILD SUPPORT AGENCY (LCSA)
Definition: The county or regional government agency that establishes parentage, obtains and modifies child support orders, locates parents, collects and distributes support, and uses enforcement tools. The LCSA represents the public interest and does not act as the personal attorney for either parent.
Explanation: The local agency helps manage and enforce child support,

but it is not either parent's private lawyer.
Example: The LCSA filed a motion to modify support after receiving updated income information from both parents.
See also: DEPARTMENT OF CHILD SUPPORT SERVICES (DCSS).

LONG TERM
Definition: Lasting for an extended period of time, usually years; in family law, long term may refer to custody arrangements, spousal support duration, or the characterization of obligations.
Explanation: Something that lasts for a long time, often years.
Example: The court established a long term visitation schedule to give the child stability.

LONG TERM MARRIAGE
Definition: Informal shorthand for a marriage of long duration. Under Family Code §4336, a marriage of 10 years or more from marriage to separation is presumed to be of long duration for purposes of retaining spousal support jurisdiction, but a shorter marriage may also qualify and a 10 year marriage does not guarantee permanent support.
Explanation: Duration can affect the court's continuing support jurisdiction, but support amount and duration still depend on the evidence and governing factors.
Example: The 15 year marriage was presumed to be of long duration, so the court retained support jurisdiction without promising that support would continue permanently.

LOW INCOME ADJUSTMENT
Definition: A rebuttable reduction built into California's child support guideline for a low income obligor. The current income range is tied to full time work at the applicable minimum wage, so the threshold can change. The court may deny the adjustment based on the statutory factors.
Explanation: The formula may reduce support for a very low income paying parent, but the reduction is not automatic in every case.
Example: The calculator showed a low income adjustment, and the judge reviewed whether applying it would still meet the child's needs.
See also: HARDSHIP DEDUCTION; CHILD SUPPORT GUIDELINE.

MAGISTRATE

Definition: A judicial officer with limited authority to conduct hearings, make findings, or issue certain orders, often under the supervision of a judge; in family law, magistrates may handle preliminary hearings, support cases, or uncontested matters.

Explanation: A court official with authority to hear and decide certain legal matters, sometimes instead of a judge.

Example: The magistrate presided over the initial child support hearing.

MANDATED REPORTER

Definition: A person required by California law to report known or reasonably suspected child abuse or neglect to the proper agency. Mandated reporters include many teachers, health professionals, therapists, child care workers, law enforcement officers, and others listed by statute.

Explanation: Certain professionals must report reasonable suspicions of child abuse; they do not wait for courtroom proof.

Example: The teacher made a mandated report after the child disclosed facts creating a reasonable suspicion of abuse.

MANDATORY

Definition: Required by law, court rule, or order; in family law, mandatory obligations may include child support payments, parenting classes, or mediation before trial.

Explanation: Something that the law or court requires and cannot be avoided.

Example: The parents attended a mandatory parenting class before their custody trial.

MANDATORY AND DISCRETIONARY SUPPORT ADD ONS

Definition: Child related expenses added to basic guideline support under Family Code §4062. Qualifying employment related child care and reasonable uninsured health care costs are mandatory. Educational or special needs expenses and travel costs for visitation are discretionary.

Explanation: Some extra child expenses must be shared, while others are shared only if the judge orders it.

Example: The court ordered both parents to share daycare and uninsured medical bills and also divided the child's special education tutoring costs.

See also: ADD ON SUPPORT - CHILD; CHILD SUPPORT ADD

ONS.

MANDATORY PARENTING CLASS
Definition: A course required by the court for divorcing or separating parents to educate them on the effects of conflict on children and encourage cooperative parenting.
Explanation: A court ordered class teaching parents how to reduce conflict and help their children during separation.
Example: Both parents had to complete a mandatory parenting class before the custody trial.

MARITAL SETTLEMENT AGREEMENT (MSA)
Definition: A written contract resolving some or all issues in a divorce or legal separation, such as property, debts, support, custody, fees, and taxes. Once approved and included in the judgment, its terms may be enforced as contract terms, judgment terms, or both, depending on the document.
Explanation: The MSA is the spouses' written divorce agreement.
Example: The parties signed an MSA dividing the home, retirement accounts, support, and tax obligations.
See also: AGREED JUDGMENT (STIPULATED JUDGMENT); SETTLEMENT; MERGER AND INCORPORATION OF AGREEMENT.

MARITAL STATUS
Definition: A person's legally recognized status regarding marriage, such as single, married, divorced, or widowed; in family law, marital status affects property rights, support, and eligibility for benefits.
Explanation: A person's legal state of being married, divorced, or single.
Example: The mother's marital status changed from married to divorced after the court's decree.

MARRIAGE CERTIFICATE
Definition: An official document issued by a government authority recording the legal union of two individuals in marriage; in family law, it is often required as proof in divorce or annulment proceedings.
Explanation: A legal paper that proves two people are married.
Example: The wife submitted a marriage certificate with her divorce petition.

MARRIAGE OF ALLEN (2002)
Definition: In re Marriage of Allen (2002) 96 Cal.App.4th 497 held that community funds used for capital improvements to one spouse's separate property are not presumed to be a gift merely because the other spouse consented; the community may be entitled to reimbursement, subject to proof and applicable property rules.
Explanation: Community money used to improve one spouse's separate property may create a reimbursement claim rather than an automatic gift.
Example: The spouse seeking reimbursement presented records showing that community funds paid for capital improvements to the other spouse's separate residence.

MARRIAGE OF FRICK (1986)
Definition: In re Marriage of Frick (1986) 181 Cal.App.3d 997 applied Moore/Marsden principles in calculating the community interest created by community payments reducing principal on separate real property. Its discussion of improvements did not establish the broad reimbursement rule stated here, and the claimed improvement reimbursement failed for lack of proof.
Explanation: Frick is principally associated with calculating the community's proportionate interest from principal reduction and appreciation under Moore/Marsden.
Example: The court used the community's principal payments and the property's appreciation to calculate the community interest in the separate property residence.

MARVIN ACTION
Definition: A civil lawsuit between unmarried partners (cohabitants) to enforce express or implied agreements regarding property division or financial support after the relationship ends. It comes from Marvin v. Marvin (1976), where the California Supreme Court held that contracts between cohabitants are enforceable if not based solely on sexual services.
Explanation: A type of lawsuit where an unmarried partner asks the court to recognize agreements or fairness in dividing property or providing support.
Example: After their breakup, the woman filed a Marvin action claiming her partner promised to share his earnings and provide lifelong support.

MATERIAL EVIDENCE
Definition: Evidence that is directly relevant and significant to the issues being decided, and that could affect the outcome of the case; in family law, material evidence may include financial records, custody evaluations, or testimony about a child's welfare.
Explanation: Important evidence that could change the judge's decision.
Example: The custody evaluator's report was considered material evidence in the case.

MATERIAL WITNESS
Definition: A witness whose testimony is considered crucial to determining the outcome of a case; in family law, a material witness might be a teacher, counselor, or doctor who can provide important insight into a child's well being.
Explanation: A very important witness whose testimony is needed for the case.
Example: The court treated the child's therapist as a material witness in the custody hearing.

MATTER
Definition: A legal dispute, issue, or subject brought before the court for resolution; in family law, a matter may refer to divorce, custody, visitation, support, or any related proceeding.
Explanation: A legal issue or case that the court must decide.
Example: The custody matter was scheduled for hearing in the family court.

MEDIATION
Definition: A process in which a neutral third party helps parents resolve disputes without a trial.
Explanation: A meeting with a neutral person to help parents agree.
Example: The couple attended mediation to settle custody issues.
See also: CHILD CUSTODY RECOMMENDING COUNSELING (CCRC); MEDIATOR; ALTERNATIVE DISPUTE RESOLUTION (ADR); COMPULSORY MEDIATION.

MEDIATOR
Definition: A neutral third party professional trained to help disputing parties reach voluntary agreements outside of court; in family law, mediators assist parents in resolving custody, visitation, and support

issues based on the best interests of the child.
Explanation: A neutral person who helps parents agree on custody, visitation, or support without a trial.
Example: The mediator helped the parents create a shared custody schedule that the court later approved.
See also: MEDIATION.

MEET AND CONFER
Definition: A good faith discussion between parties or attorneys to narrow or resolve a dispute before asking the court to intervene. Discovery motions and many local family law procedures require a meaningful meet and confer, not only a form letter.
Explanation: The sides must honestly try to solve the problem before filing certain motions.
Example: Counsel met by video, exchanged proposed search terms, and resolved most of the document dispute before filing the motion to compel.
See also: MOTION TO COMPEL.

MENTAL INCAPACITY
Definition: A lack of legal capacity to perform a particular act or make a particular decision. Capacity is decision specific and depends on the applicable statute and evidence; a diagnosis of mental illness or cognitive impairment does not by itself establish incapacity for every purpose.
Explanation: The court asks whether the person could understand and appreciate the particular decision at the relevant time.
Example: The court considered medical and other evidence about whether the spouse understood the nature and effect of the agreement when it was signed.

MENTALLY ILL
Definition: A dated and potentially stigmatizing phrase for a person with a mental illness. In family law, a diagnosis alone does not determine custody or parental fitness; the relevant question is whether symptoms or conduct actually affect the child's health, safety, welfare, or the person's ability to participate in the proceeding.
Explanation: Courts should focus on actual functioning, safety, treatment, and parenting conduct rather than a label.
Example: The court considered how the parent's current symptoms and treatment affected caregiving rather than treating the diagnosis alone as

proof of unfitness.

MERGER AND INCORPORATION OF AGREEMENT
Definition: Terms describing how a settlement agreement becomes part of a judgment. An incorporated agreement is included or referenced in the judgment. A merged agreement loses separate contract status to the extent of merger and is enforced as a judgment; nonmerged terms may retain contract remedies.
Explanation: Whether the agreement merges into the judgment can affect how it is enforced later.
Example: The judgment stated that the custody and support terms merged, while a separate property promise was incorporated but not merged.
See also: MARITAL SETTLEMENT AGREEMENT (MSA).

MERITS
Definition: The actual facts and substantive legal issues of a case, as opposed to technical or procedural matters; in family law, decisions on the merits focus on evidence regarding custody, support, or property division.
Explanation: The real issues and evidence in a case, not just the technical rules.
Example: The judge ruled on the merits of the custody dispute, emphasizing the child's best interests.

MILITARY RETIRED PAY - 10/10 RULE
Definition: A federal payment rule allowing the Defense Finance and Accounting Service to pay a former spouse's awarded share of military retired pay directly when the marriage and the member's creditable military service overlapped by at least 10 years. It does not decide whether the retirement benefit is community property.
Explanation: The 10/10 rule concerns direct federal payment, not whether a shorter marriage can receive a share of the pension.
Example: The former spouse received a pension share under state law, but DFAS direct payment was unavailable because military service overlapped the marriage for only eight years.
See also: FROZEN BENEFIT RULE - MILITARY RETIRED PAY; SURVIVOR BENEFIT.

MINIMUM PAYMENT
Definition: The lowest amount a party is legally required to pay at a given time toward a debt or obligation; in family law, this may refer to ordered child support, spousal support, or payment plans for arrears.
Explanation: The smallest amount a person must pay to stay current on a debt or support order.
Example: The father was ordered to make a minimum payment each month toward his child support arrears.

MINOR
Definition: A person under the age of majority, usually under 18, who is subject to parental authority or court jurisdiction.
Explanation: A child under 18 years old.
Example: The court appointed a guardian for the minor.

MINOR'S COUNSEL
Definition: An attorney appointed to represent a child in a custody or visitation case. Minor's counsel gathers and presents admissible evidence, protects the child's rights, and states the child's wishes when appropriate. The attorney does not serve as the judge's witness or as a custody evaluator.
Explanation: The child's lawyer represents the child, not either parent and not the court.
Example: Minor's counsel reviewed school and medical records and told the court the mature child's wishes about the schedule.
See also: RULE 5.250 CHILD PARTICIPATION; IN CAMERA INTERVIEW OF CHILD.

MINUTE ORDER
Definition: A written court record, usually prepared by the clerk, summarizing what occurred and what the court ordered at a hearing. A minute order may be enforceable, but a later signed order or judgment may provide fuller or controlling terms, depending on the case.
Explanation: It is the clerk's written record of the judge's rulings from the hearing.
Example: The parties used the minute order to follow the temporary exchange schedule while the formal FOAH was being prepared.
See also: COURT ORDER.

MISLEADING
Definition: A statement, action, or piece of evidence that has the tendency to deceive or create a false impression, whether intentional or not; in family law, misleading information may arise in financial disclosures, testimony, or representations made to the court.
Explanation: Information that gives the wrong idea or hides the truth.
Example: The court found the father's income statement misleading because he failed to include his overtime pay.

MISSTATES THE EVIDENCE
Definition: An objection that a question or argument inaccurately describes testimony, a document, or another item already admitted. The judge may direct the questioner to use the witness's actual words or the exhibit's accurate contents.
Explanation: The lawyer is describing the evidence incorrectly.
Example: Counsel said the witness saw Father strike the child, but the witness had testified only that she heard a noise, so the objection was sustained.

MISTRIAL
Definition: A trial that is declared invalid before its conclusion because of a fundamental error, misconduct, or inability of the jury or judge to proceed fairly; in family law, mistrials are rare but may occur if key evidence was improperly admitted or due process was violated.
Explanation: A trial that must be stopped and treated as if it never happened because of a serious problem.
Example: The judge declared a mistrial in the custody case after learning that confidential records had been improperly shared.

MODIFICATION
Definition: A legal request to change an existing court order, often for custody, visitation, or support.
Explanation: Asking the court to change an existing order.
Example: He filed a modification to reduce his child support.
See also: CUSTODY MODIFICATION; MOTION TO MODIFY SUPPORT.

MONEY JUDGMENT
Definition: A court's formal order requiring one party to pay a specific sum of money to another, often arising from arrears in child support,

spousal support, or damages; enforceable through collection tools like wage garnishment or liens.
Explanation: A judge's order that someone must pay money to another person.
Example: The mother obtained a money judgment against the father for $10,000 in unpaid child support.
See also: ARREARAGE (ARREARS).

MONITORED EXCHANGE
Definition: A custody exchange supervised by a neutral third party to ensure the safety of the child and parents.
Explanation: When someone watches while parents switch custody of the child.
Example: The parents used a monitored exchange center to avoid direct confrontation.
See also: CHILD EXCHANGE PROGRAM (NEUTRAL SITE); CUSTODY SWAP LOCATION.

MONTENEGRO CHANGED CIRCUMSTANCES RULE
Definition: A custody rule from Montenegro v. Diaz. After a final judicial custody determination, the parent seeking a change generally must show a significant change of circumstances that may make a new custody order necessary for the child's best interests. A temporary order, or an agreement that does not clearly show finality, may not trigger this rule.
Explanation: Once a custody order is truly final, the parent asking to change it usually must show an important new change affecting the child.
Example: The court found the earlier order was temporary, so Mother did not have to meet the Montenegro changed circumstances rule before the court reconsidered custody.
See also: CUSTODY MODIFICATION.

MONTHLY PAYMENT
Definition: A regularly scheduled sum of money due each month to satisfy a legal obligation, such as child support, spousal support, or payment toward arrears.
Explanation: The amount someone must pay every month under a court order.
Example: The father was ordered to make a monthly payment of $750 in child support.

MOORE/MARSDEN
Definition: A California family law principle, from Marriage of Moore and Marriage of Marsden, that gives the community (marital estate) a proportional ownership interest in real property purchased before marriage but paid down with marital funds.
Explanation: A rule in California divorce law that splits part of a house's value when marital money was used to pay for property owned before marriage.
Example: The judge applied the Moore/Marsden formula to divide the equity in the husband's premarital home.

MORAL TURPITUDE
Definition: Conduct that is considered contrary to community standards of honesty, morality, or good morals; in family law, findings of crimes involving moral turpitude may affect custody or parental rights.
Explanation: Behavior considered dishonest, immoral, or very wrong.
Example: The father's conviction for a crime of moral turpitude was raised in the custody hearing.

MORRISON RULE
Definition: A spousal support principle from In re Marriage of Morrison that cautions against ending support jurisdiction at an arbitrary future date after a long marriage when future self support is uncertain. The court should base termination on evidence, not speculation.
Explanation: After a long marriage, the court should not guess that the supported spouse will be self supporting by a fixed date without solid evidence.
Example: The appellate court reversed a support cutoff that assumed Wife would earn enough within two years despite no evidence supporting that prediction.
See also: RICHMOND ORDER; GAVRON WARNING.

MOTION
Definition: A formal written or oral request asking the court to issue a ruling or order on a specific issue during a case; in family law, motions may request temporary custody, modification of support, or protective orders.
Explanation: A request made to the judge to decide on a particular issue in the case.
Example: The mother filed a motion to modify visitation after the father

relocated.

MOTION FOR RECONSIDERATION
Definition: A strictly limited request asking the same court to reconsider an earlier order under Code of Civil Procedure § 1008 because of new or different facts, circumstances, or law. The moving party must act within the statutory time and explain why the new material was not presented earlier.
Explanation: A party asks the judge to look again at an order because something important and genuinely new has arisen.
Example: Mother timely sought reconsideration after receiving a newly issued school safety report that was unavailable at the first hearing.

MOTION IN LIMINE
Definition: A request made before or during trial asking the court to admit, exclude, or limit particular evidence or argument. The motion should identify the specific evidence and legal ground and should not be used as a vague request to follow the law. Motions in Limine are rarely used in family law cases because trials are heard by a judge instead of by a jury.
Explanation: The motion asks the judge to decide an evidence issue before it disrupts the trial.
Example: Father filed a motion in limine to exclude an unauthenticated recording and any reference to it during opening statement.
See also: EVIDENCE CODE SECTION 352 OBJECTION; OFFER OF PROOF; OBJECTION.

MOTION TO COMPEL
Definition: A request asking the court to order a party or nonparty to provide discovery, answer questions, produce documents, attend a deposition, or obey a subpoena. Strict filing deadlines, meet and confer duties, separate statements, and sanctions rules may apply.
Explanation: A party asks the judge to force the other side to provide required information.
Example: Wife moved to compel after Husband gave no bank records and ignored a detailed meet and confer letter.
See also: DISCOVERY SANCTIONS; MEET AND CONFER.

MOTION TO MODIFY SUPPORT
Definition: A legal request asking the court to change an existing child

or spousal support order due to changed circumstances such as income or needs.
Explanation: Asking the court to change support payments because of new circumstances.
Example: The father filed a motion to modify support after losing his job.
See also: CHANGE OF CIRCUMSTANCES; SUPPORT RETROACTIVITY; MODIFICATION.

MOVE AWAY CASE
Definition: A custody case involving a proposed move that would significantly affect the existing parenting arrangement. The legal test depends on whether the current order is temporary or final and whether custody is sole or joint. The child's best interests and possible detriment remain central.
Explanation: A move away case decides whether and how a child may relocate when the move would make the current schedule hard to continue.
Example: Mother asked to move the child 500 miles, and the court held a move away trial to decide custody and a new long distance schedule.
See also: BURGESS RULE; LAMUSGA FACTORS; RELOCATION.

MUTUAL RESTRAINING ORDERS
Definition: Court orders issued against both parties in a family law case, prohibiting harassment, threats, or contact between them.
Explanation: Orders stopping both people in a case from harassing or threatening each other.
Example: The judge issued mutual restraining orders during the divorce proceedings.

NAME CHANGE PETITION (FAMILY COURT)
Definition: A request for a legal name change. In California, an adult or child generally uses a separate name change petition in the superior court; a spouse may request restoration of a former name within a dissolution case, and an adoption order may also support a name change. The proper procedure depends on the reason and case type.
Explanation: Most name changes use a separate court process, while divorce and adoption have specialized procedures.
Example: The parent filed a separate petition in the superior court to change the child's name and gave the other parent the required notice.

NEGLECT
Definition: Failure of a parent or guardian to provide necessary care, supervision, or support for a child.
Explanation: When a parent doesn't give a child the care they need.
Example: The agency investigated a claim of neglect.

NEGLIGENCE
Definition: The failure to exercise the care that a reasonably prudent person would in similar circumstances, resulting in harm or risk of harm; in family law, negligence may involve failing to provide proper care, supervision, or safety for a child.
Explanation: When someone does not act carefully enough and puts another person, often a child, at risk.
Example: The court considered the mother's negligence in leaving the child unattended when deciding custody.

NET DISPOSABLE INCOME
Definition: Income remaining after the deductions allowed by child support statutes, such as taxes, mandatory retirement contributions, health insurance premiums, and other permitted deductions. It is not always the same as take home pay shown on a paycheck.
Explanation: The support formula starts with income and subtracts only deductions the law allows.
Example: The court added back a voluntary payroll deduction that was not allowed when calculating Father's net disposable income.
See also: CHILD SUPPORT GUIDELINE; SELF EMPLOYMENT INCOME; GROSS WAGES; NEW MATE INCOME EXCLUSION.

NEW MATE INCOME EXCLUSION
Definition: The general rule that the income of a parent's new spouse or nonmarital partner is not considered when setting or modifying child support, except in an extraordinary case where excluding it would cause extreme and severe hardship to a child. The new partner's income can still affect tax calculations in limited ways.
Explanation: A new spouse usually does not become responsible for a parent's child support from another relationship.
Example: The court did not count Mother's new husband's salary as her income in the guideline calculation.
See also: CHILD SUPPORT GUIDELINE; NET DISPOSABLE INCOME.

NO CONTACT ORDER
Definition: A court order prohibiting one person from directly or indirectly communicating with or approaching another; in family law, no contact orders are often issued in domestic violence cases to protect spouses, partners, or children.
Explanation: A judge's order that stops someone from calling, messaging, or approaching another person.
Example: The court issued a no contact order preventing the father from contacting the mother outside of custody exchanges.
See also: RESTRAINING ORDER.

NO FAULT DIVORCE
Definition: A divorce that does not require proof of wrongdoing by either spouse, often based on irreconcilable differences.
Explanation: Divorce without blaming either spouse.
Example: They filed for a no fault divorce citing irreconcilable differences.

NONCOMPLIANCE
Definition: The failure or refusal to follow a court order, law, or legal requirement; in family law, noncompliance may involve not paying child support, not following custody or visitation schedules, or ignoring restraining orders.
Explanation: When someone does not do what the court has ordered.
Example: The judge found the father in noncompliance for failing to pay three months of child support.

NONCUSTODIAL PARENT
Definition: A parent who does not have primary physical custody but may retain legal custody and parenting time rights.
Explanation: The parent the child doesn't mainly live with.
Example: The noncustodial parent has visitation rights.
See also: CUSTODIAL PARENT.

NONMARITAL CHILD SUPPORT
Definition: Financial support ordered for a child whose parents were never married, calculated the same way as for children of married parents.
Explanation: Child support for children of parents who were not married.
Example: The father was ordered to pay nonmarital child support after

paternity was established.

NONMODIFIABLE SPOUSAL SUPPORT

Definition: Spousal support that the parties have validly agreed cannot be changed or ended by the court, except as the agreement itself permits. Clear written language is normally required because support is otherwise subject to statutory modification rules.
Explanation: The court cannot later change support when the spouses clearly and validly agreed that it would be nonmodifiable.
Example: The MSA stated that support of $2,000 per month for three years was nonmodifiable as to amount and duration.

NONRESPONSIVE ANSWER

Definition: An objection or request to strike when a witness's answer does not address the question asked. The judge may direct the witness to answer, but relevant additional information may be allowed if it fairly explains the response.
Explanation: The witness did not answer the question and began discussing something else.
Example: When asked for the exchange time, Father described the entire marriage, so the judge directed him to give a responsive answer.

NOTARIZE

Definition: To have a notary public officially certify the authenticity of a signature on a document, confirming the signer's identity and willingness; in family law, documents such as affidavits, adoption consents, or property agreements may need to be notarized.
Explanation: When a notary officially confirms that a signature on a legal paper is real.
Example: The parents had to notarize their custody agreement before filing it with the court.

NOTARY PUBLIC

Definition: An official authorized by the state to witness signatures, administer oaths, and certify documents; in family law, a notary public ensures the validity of consents, waivers, and sworn statements.
Explanation: An official who verifies signatures and documents for legal purposes.
Example: The adoption papers were signed in front of a notary public.

NOTICE

Definition: A formal written communication informing a party of legal action, hearing, or court order, required to ensure due process; in family law, notice must be properly served to the other party.
Explanation: An official paper that tells someone about a case or hearing.
Example: The father received notice of the upcoming custody hearing.

NOTICE OF APPEAL

Definition: A written filing submitted to start an appeal, informing the court and opposing party that the filer seeks review of a judgment; in family law, a notice of appeal is the first step in challenging orders regarding custody, support, or divorce.
Explanation: The paper filed to tell the court you want to appeal a decision.
Example: The mother filed a notice of appeal to challenge the child custody order.
See also: APPEAL.

NOTICE OF ENTRY OF JUDGMENT OR ORDER

Definition: Formal notice that a judgment or appealable order has been entered. Proper service can start the shorter deadline for filing a notice of appeal, while the outside deadline may be longer if no qualifying notice is served. The exact deadline depends on the order and appellate rules.
Explanation: This notice can start the clock for an appeal, so the service date is important.
Example: After receiving notice of entry of the support order, Husband calendared the deadline for any appeal.

NOTICE OF HEARING

Definition: A formal document notifying parties of the date, time, and place of a scheduled court hearing; in family law, proper notice of hearing is required for motions, custody disputes, and support hearings.
Explanation: A paper that tells the parties when and where the hearing will be.
Example: The clerk mailed the notice of hearing to both parents regarding the support modification.

NOTICE OF RELOCATION

Definition: Advance notice of a proposed change in a child's residence

when required by a custody order or other law. Under Family Code section 3024, a custody order may require notice to the other parent before a change lasting more than 30 days, generally with sufficient advance time for mediation or court review; the notice is not necessarily a document filed with the court.
Explanation: The moving parent may have to give written advance notice to the other parent, and a disputed move may require a request to modify custody.
Example: The parent mailed the advance notice required by the custody order and filed a Request for Order when the proposed move required a new parenting plan.
See also: RELOCATION.

NOTICE TO CONSUMER

Definition: Advance notice required before certain subpoenas seek a consumer's personal records from a third party, such as bank, employment, medical, or educational records. The consumer has a limited time to object or move to quash before the records are produced.
Explanation: A person usually must be warned before private records are obtained from a business or provider.
Example: Father served Mother with a notice to consumer before subpoenaing her bank records.

NUNC PRO TUNC ORDER

Definition: An order entered now to make the written record correctly reflect a judicial act that was actually taken earlier. It may correct a clerical omission or error, but it generally cannot be used to create a new substantive ruling retroactively.
Explanation: The court can correct the record to show what it already decided, but cannot pretend it made a decision that never occurred.
Example: The judge entered a nunc pro tunc correction because the signed order accidentally omitted the termination date stated in open court.

OATH

Definition: A solemn promise, often made before a judge or notary, to tell the truth or faithfully carry out duties, with penalties for perjury if broken; in family law, parties, witnesses, and interpreters give oaths before testifying.
Explanation: A promise to tell the truth or do one's duty, made formally

in court.
Example: The witness took an oath before testifying about the child's living arrangements.

OBJECT

Definition: To formally oppose evidence, testimony, or procedure during a court proceeding, usually on legal grounds such as relevance or hearsay; in family law, objections protect parties from improper evidence being considered.
Explanation: To tell the judge you disagree with something presented in court and want it excluded.
Example: The attorney raised an objection when the opposing party attempted to introduce hearsay evidence.

OBJECTION

Definition: A formal request asking the court to exclude, limit, or correct improper evidence, testimony, argument, or procedure.
Explanation: When a lawyer tells the judge that something should not be allowed.
Example: The attorney made an objection to the hearsay testimony.
See also: MOTION IN LIMINE; OVERRULE; STRIKE.

OFF THE RECORD

Definition: A statement, discussion, or exchange that is not included in the official transcript of a court proceeding; in family law, judges or attorneys may go off the record for informal discussions, but these do not become part of the case history.
Explanation: Something said in court but not officially recorded as part of the case.
Example: The judge spoke with both attorneys off the record to encourage settlement discussions.

OFFER OF PROOF

Definition: A statement explaining what excluded or unavailable evidence would show and why it is admissible and important. An offer of proof helps the trial judge rule and helps preserve an evidence issue for appellate review.
Explanation: The party tells the judge what the witness or exhibit would prove so the issue is clear for the record.
Example: Counsel offered to prove that the teacher would testify to 30

documented absences during Mother's custodial time.
See also: MOTION IN LIMINE.

OMITTED ASSET OR DEBT
Definition: A community asset or liability that was not decided in the original judgment. Family Code §2556 gives the court continuing power to divide the omitted item, usually equally unless the interests of justice require a different division.
Explanation: Property or debt missed in the divorce can still be divided later.
Example: Years after judgment, the court divided an undisclosed pension as an omitted asset.
See also: CONTINUING DUTY OF DISCLOSURE; PRELIMINARY DECLARATION OF DISCLOSURE; FINAL DECLARATION OF DISCLOSURE.

ON OR ABOUT
Definition: A legal phrase used to indicate that an event happened approximately on a certain date, without requiring exact precision; in family law, this is often used in pleadings and testimony.
Explanation: A way of saying that something happened around a specific date, not exactly on it.
Example: The petition alleged that the father stopped paying support on or about June 1.

ON THE RECORD
Definition: Statements, evidence, or proceedings that are officially transcribed and form part of the case's legal history; in family law, everything said on the record may be reviewed on appeal.
Explanation: Something said in court that is officially recorded as part of the case.
Example: The mother wanted her objection placed on the record to preserve it for appeal.

OPENING ARGUMENTS
Definition: A nonpreferred phrase for opening statements. At the start of trial, each side may outline what the evidence is expected to show; an opening statement is not evidence and ordinarily should not argue facts that will not be supported.
Explanation: The proper term is usually "opening statement," which

previews the expected evidence rather than serving as closing argument.
Example: In the opening statement, counsel described the evidence expected from the parents, teacher, and custody evaluator.

OPENING STATEMENT
Definition: Similar to an opening argument, it is a formal presentation at the start of trial summarizing what each party expects the evidence will show; in family law, opening statements prepare the judge to understand the custody or support issues at stake.
Explanation: A short overview at the beginning of trial about what each side will try to prove.
Example: The mother's attorney gave an opening statement explaining why sole custody served the child's best interests.

OPINION
Definition: A written explanation by a judge or Appellate Court setting forth the reasoning behind a decision; in family law, opinions may interpret custody statutes, support guidelines, or constitutional rights.
Explanation: A judge's written explanation of why they made their decision.
Example: The appellate court's opinion explained why the custody ruling was affirmed.

ORDER
Definition: A written or spoken command issued by a court or judge requiring action or forbidding it.
Explanation: A judge's official instruction.
Example: The judge issued an order granting visitation rights.

ORDER SHORTENING TIME (OST)
Definition: An order reducing the normal notice, filing, service, or response time for a request for order. The requesting party must show facts supporting faster treatment. An OST is different from relief without notice because the other side may still receive notice and a chance to respond.
Explanation: The judge speeds up the normal motion schedule because the issue cannot reasonably wait.
Example: The court shortened time so a school enrollment dispute could be heard before classes began.

ORDER TO SHOW CAUSE (OSC)

Definition: A court order requiring a party to appear and explain why the court should not take a proposed action.
Explanation: A notice telling someone to come to court and explain themselves.
Example: The judge issued an order to show cause in the custody matter.

ORDINANCE

Definition: A law or regulation enacted by a city, county, or other local government authority; in family law, ordinances may relate to housing, zoning, domestic partnerships, or local protections against harassment and abuse.
Explanation: A local law made by a city or county.
Example: The court referenced a county ordinance requiring background checks for child care providers.

OSTLER-SMITH ORDER

Definition: A support order requiring a stated percentage of future bonuses, commissions, overtime, distributions, or other fluctuating income as additional child or spousal support. The percentage should be tied to the support analysis and the order should explain reporting, payment, and any cap or reconciliation terms.
Explanation: A base support amount is paid each month, plus a percentage when extra income is received.
Example: Husband paid monthly support and 12 percent of each gross bonus within 10 days after receiving it.

OUTSTANDING DEBTS

Definition: Financial obligations that remain unpaid at the time of legal proceedings; in family law, outstanding debts acquired during the marriage may be considered community or marital debts and divided between spouses.
Explanation: Money that is still owed and has not yet been paid off.
Example: The divorce decree required the couple to divide their outstanding debts equally, including loans and credit cards.

OVERRULE

Definition: A judicial ruling that rejects an objection raised during a hearing or trial, allowing the evidence or testimony to be admitted; in

appellate practice, to overrule also means to reverse or set aside a prior precedent.
Explanation: When the judge rejects a lawyer's objection and lets the evidence or testimony in.
Example: The father's attorney objected to the testimony, but the judge overruled the objection and allowed it.
See also: OBJECTION.

PAIN AND SUFFERING
Definition: A category of damages awarded for physical discomfort, emotional distress, or mental anguish caused by wrongful acts; in family law, claims for pain and suffering may arise in cases involving domestic violence or intentional infliction of emotional harm.
Explanation: Money a court may order as compensation for physical or emotional harm.
Example: The mother sought damages for pain and suffering caused by years of domestic abuse.

PALIMONY
Definition: A slang term for financial support claimed by one unmarried partner from another after the end of a cohabiting relationship, based on contract or equitable principles rather than family law statutes.
Explanation: Support money (like alimony) requested by an unmarried partner after separation, but based on an agreement or fairness.
Example: She sued for palimony, arguing her partner had promised to support her even though they never married.

PARENT
Definition: A person who has a legally recognized parent child relationship, whether through birth, adoption, presumption, voluntary declaration, assisted reproduction law, or court judgment. Legal parentage carries rights and responsibilities concerning care, custody, association, and support.
Explanation: A legal parent may be established in several ways and is not limited to a biological mother or father.
Example: The court determined that both parents would share legal custody of the child.

PARENTAGE BY HOLDING OUT
Definition: A presumed parent basis under Family Code §7611 when a

person receives a child into the person's home and openly holds the child out as the person's natural child. The court examines conduct, commitment, family understanding, and the parent child relationship, not only biology.
Explanation: A person who lives with, raises, and publicly treats a child as their own may become a presumed parent.
Example: The court found presumed parentage after the nonbiological parent raised the child from birth and was known at school and in the community as a parent.
See also: PRESUMED PARENT; COMPETING PARENTAGE PRESUMPTIONS.

PARENTAGE JUDGMENT SET ASIDE
Definition: A statutory procedure for setting aside certain parentage judgments when genetic testing shows that a previously established father is not the genetic father. Strict deadlines, exclusions, and best interest considerations apply, and the procedure does not cover every parentage status or assisted reproduction case.
Explanation: A person may challenge some parentage judgments with genetic evidence, but the law has narrow limits and short deadlines.
Example: The previously established father filed within two years after learning of the judgment and requested court ordered genetic testing.

PARENTAL KIDNAPPING PREVENTION ACT (PKPA)
Definition: A federal law requiring states to honor qualifying child custody orders from other states and limiting when another state may modify them. The PKPA works with the UCCJEA but is federal law and controls if the two conflict.
Explanation: Federal law helps prevent competing custody orders from different states.
Example: The California court declined to modify the valid Colorado order because Colorado still had jurisdiction under the PKPA.
See also: UNIFORM CHILD CUSTODY JURISDICTION AND ENFORCEMENT ACT (UCCJEA); FULL FAITH AND CREDIT FOR PROTECTIVE ORDERS.

PARENTAL RIGHTS
Definition: The legal rights and responsibilities of parents concerning a child's care, custody, decision making, association, and support.
Explanation: The legal powers and duties parents have over children.

Example: The court discussed terminating parental rights in the adoption case.

PARENTING COURSE
Definition: A court ordered educational program designed to teach parents effective communication, conflict resolution, and strategies to minimize the negative impact of divorce or separation on children; many jurisdictions require parenting courses in custody or divorce cases before final orders are entered.
Explanation: A class parents must take to learn how to help their children during divorce or custody disputes.
Example: The judge required both parents to complete a parenting course before finalizing the custody arrangement.

PARENTING PLAN
Definition: A written agreement or court order allocating legal decision making responsibilities, parenting time, exchanges, holidays, and related child care arrangements.
Explanation: A plan that explains custody and visitation details for the child.
Example: The parents submitted a parenting plan to the court.
See also: PARENTING TIME; AGREED PARENTING PLAN; VISITATION SCHEDULE.

PARENTING SKILLS EVALUATION
Definition: An assessment of a parent's ability to provide proper care, discipline, and support for their child, often ordered in custody disputes.
Explanation: An evaluation to see if a parent has the skills to care for a child properly.
Example: The judge ordered a parenting skills evaluation before deciding custody.

PARENTING TIME
Definition: The schedule specifying when a child is in each parent's care; in jurisdictions using this terminology, it replaces visitation and the scheduling component of physical custody.
Explanation: The term emphasizes each parent's time and responsibilities. California statutes still principally use custody and visitation, although courts and practitioners also use parenting time.
Example: The divorce decree gave the father parenting time every other

weekend and one evening per week.
See also: CHILD CUSTODY; CUSTODY; LEGAL DECISION MAKING; VISITATION; PARENTING PLAN.

PARTIES
Definition: The individuals or entities directly involved in a legal case who have legal rights and obligations in the proceedings; in family law, parties typically include spouses, parents, or guardians.
Explanation: The people who are part of a legal case.
Example: The court reminded the parties that the custody hearing was about the child's best interests, not personal grievances.

PARTY
Definition: A single individual or entity that takes part in a legal case; in family law, a party may be a spouse, parent, or guardian involved in proceedings concerning divorce, custody, support, or adoption.
Explanation: One person who is officially part of a court case.
Example: The father was named as a party in the child custody proceedings.

PATERNITY
Definition: The legal determination of fatherhood through presumption, acknowledgment, genetic evidence, or a court judgment establishing parentage.
Explanation: The legal process of deciding who the father is.
Example: The mother filed a case to establish paternity.
See also: VOLUNTARY DECLARATION OF PARENTAGE (VDOP); DNA; PRESUMED PARENT.

PAYABLE
Definition: A financial obligation that is due to be paid, either immediately or at a set date, often referenced in judgments or support orders.
Explanation: Money that must be paid under a court order.
Example: Child support was payable on the first of each month.

PAYMENT
Definition: The transfer of money or value to satisfy a legal obligation; in family law, payments typically include child support, spousal support, or reimbursement of expenses.

Explanation: Money given to meet a court ordered duty.
Example: The father made his monthly child support payment on time.

PENALTY
Definition: A punishment, fine, or consequence imposed for violating a law or court order; in family law, penalties may include fines for contempt or sanctions for late support payments.
Explanation: Consequences for breaking the law or ignoring a court order.
Example: The court imposed a penalty for failure to follow the visitation schedule.

PENALTY OF PERJURY
Definition: A statement made under oath that the signer affirms is true, with the risk of criminal penalties if the statement is false.
Explanation: Signing or declaring something as true, with punishment if it turns out false.
Example: The financial disclosure form was signed under penalty of perjury.

PENDENTE LITE
Definition: A Latin phrase meaning 'while the case is pending.' It usually describes temporary orders for custody, support, attorney's fees, property control, or other needs before final judgment.
Explanation: The order is temporary and lasts during the lawsuit.
Example: The court entered a pendente lite spousal support order that remained in effect until trial or further order.

PENDING
Definition: Describing a case, motion, or issue that has been filed or raised but has not yet been finally decided.
Explanation: A case that has been started but not yet finished.
Example: The custody case is still pending before the family court.

PEREIRA METHOD
Definition: A method used in California family law to divide community and separate property interests in a business when community labor has significantly increased its value. The Pereira method allocates a fair rate of return on the separate property investment, and the remainder of the growth is treated as community property. It comes from Pereira v.

Pereira (1909).
Explanation: A way to divide a business in divorce: the original investment stays separate, but most of the increase in value from work during the marriage is shared.
Example: The court applied the Pereira method, awarding the husband a return on his original investment and classifying the rest of the business growth as community property.
See also: VAN CAMP METHOD; BUSINESS VALUATION; PROFESSIONAL GOODWILL.

PEREMPTORY CHALLENGE

Definition: The right of a party to reject a potential juror without stating a reason, limited in number by statute or rule. Rare in family law, since most trials are bench trials.
Explanation: The right to excuse a juror without giving a reason.
Example: During jury selection in a family related tort case, the attorney exercised a peremptory challenge.

PERJURY

Definition: The criminal offense of knowingly making a false statement under oath in a judicial proceeding.
Explanation: Lying under oath in court or in sworn documents.
Example: The mother faced charges of perjury for lying in her affidavit about her income.

PERMANENT GUARDIANSHIP

Definition: A long term order giving a guardian legal custody and decision making rights for a child until adulthood, without terminating parental rights.
Explanation: When a guardian gets long term legal custody of a child until adulthood.
Example: The aunt was granted permanent guardianship after repeated parental neglect.

PERSONAL PROPERTY

Definition: Movable property owned by a person, not including land or buildings; in family law, personal property may be divided during divorce.
Explanation: Belongings other than land or houses, such as cars, jewelry, or furniture.
Example: The divorce decree divided personal property, giving the

mother the family car.

PET PROTECTION ORDER
Definition: A domestic violence protective order term giving a protected party exclusive care, possession, or control of an animal and ordering the restrained party to stay away from or not harm, hide, transfer, or dispose of the animal.
Explanation: A DVRO can protect a family pet as well as people.
Example: The order gave Wife possession of the dog and required Husband to stay 100 yards away from the animal.
See also: DOMESTIC VIOLENCE RESTRAINING ORDER.

PETITION
Definition: A formal written pleading asking a court to begin a proceeding and grant specified legal relief.
Explanation: A legal paper asking the court to decide on an issue.
Example: The father filed a petition for joint custody.

PETITIONER
Definition: The party who starts a legal proceeding by filing a petition and requesting relief from the court.
Explanation: The person who starts a case in court.
Example: The petitioner asked for spousal support in addition to custody.

PIQUI'S LAW
Definition: California legislation that strengthened child safety training in custody and domestic violence matters and added Family Code §3193. That section bars courts from ordering certain coercive family reunification programs that require no contact, multiday or out of state stays, custody transfers, private transport using force, or other acutely distressing tactics.
Explanation: A court cannot force a child into specified reunification camps or programs that use isolation, forced transport, custody transfer, or similar coercion.
Example: The judge refused a proposed out of state reunification program because it required forced transport and a no contact period prohibited by Section 3193.
See also: REUNIFICATION COUNSELING.

PLACEMENT
Definition: The arrangement of where a child will live, either temporarily or permanently, by court order.
Explanation: The decision of where a child will live.
Example: The court ordered placement of the child with relatives during the investigation.

PLAINTIFF
Definition: The party who begins a civil lawsuit by filing a complaint against one or more defendants.
Explanation: The person who starts a case asking the court for relief.
Example: The plaintiff filed a related civil action for damages; in the dissolution case, the initiating party was called the petitioner.

PLEADINGS
Definition: Formal written court filings stating the parties' claims, defenses, admissions, denials, and requested legal relief.
Explanation: The written papers that tell the court each side's position.
Example: The pleadings in the custody case included allegations of neglect.

POSSESSION
Definition: The control or holding of property, either physical or legal; in family law, it may refer to temporary possession of a marital home or belongings.
Explanation: Having or controlling property.
Example: The mother was given temporary possession of the family residence.

POST ADOPTION CONTACT AGREEMENT
Definition: An agreement between birth parents and adoptive parents that allows some form of contact or communication after adoption.
Explanation: A deal that lets birth parents stay in touch with the child after adoption.
Example: The birth mother signed a post adoption contact agreement allowing yearly visits.

POSTPONE
Definition: To delay or reschedule a hearing, trial, deadline, or required legal act to a later time.

Explanation: To move a hearing or requirement to a later date.
Example: The court agreed to postpone the child support hearing.

POWER OF ATTORNEY
Definition: A legal document granting one person authority to act on behalf of another; in family law, this may be used for child care, financial management, or medical decisions.
Explanation: A paper giving someone else legal power to act for you.
Example: The mother signed a power of attorney allowing her sister to care for the child during deployment.

PREJUDICE
Definition: In legal terms, harm or disadvantage caused by a ruling; in family law, a case dismissed "with prejudice" cannot be refiled, while "without prejudice" allows refiling.
Explanation: Whether a case can be brought back again after dismissal.
Example: The judge dismissed the petition with prejudice due to lack of evidence.

PRELIMINARY DECLARATION OF DISCLOSURE
Definition: The early mandatory financial exchange in a California dissolution or legal separation. Each spouse serves a disclosure declaration, an income and expense declaration, and complete schedules of assets, debts, and material facts. The preliminary disclosure generally cannot be waived.
Explanation: Early in the case, each spouse must give the other a full financial picture.
Example: Wife served her preliminary disclosure with bank statements, property values, debts, and current income information.
See also: OMITTED ASSET OR DEBT; FELDMAN DISCLOSURE SANCTIONS; SCHEDULE OF ASSETS AND DEBTS (FL-142).

PREMARITAL AGREEMENT SEVEN-DAY RULE
Definition: For agreements governed by the current California rule, at least seven calendar days must pass between the date a party is first presented with the final agreement and the date the agreement is signed. The rule generally applies even when the party has independent counsel.
Explanation: A person must receive the final premarital agreement at least seven days before signing it.
Example: The couple postponed signing because the final draft was first

delivered only three days before the wedding.
See also: UNIFORM PREMARITAL AGREEMENT ACT / SECTION 1615; PREMARITAL SPOUSAL SUPPORT WAIVER.

PREMARITAL SPOUSAL SUPPORT WAIVER
Definition: A premarital agreement term limiting or waiving future spousal support. Under California law, the waiver is not enforceable against a party who lacked independent counsel when signing, and it may also be unenforceable if unconscionable when enforcement is sought.
Explanation: A prenup can address future support, but California requires a lawyer and allows a fairness review at the time of divorce.
Example: The court declined to enforce the support waiver because Wife had no independent attorney when she signed the agreement.
See also: PREMARITAL AGREEMENT SEVEN-DAY RULE.

PREPONDERANCE OF THE EVIDENCE
Definition: The standard of proof in most civil and family law cases, requiring that a fact be more likely true than not (greater than 50%).
Explanation: The level of proof showing something is more likely true than not.
Example: The court used the preponderance of the evidence standard to decide the custody dispute.

PRESCRIBED
Definition: Required, directed, or established by a statute, court rule, judicial order, or other governing authority.
Explanation: Something required by the law or judge.
Example: The parents completed the prescribed parenting class before finalizing their divorce.

PRESIDING JUDGE
Definition: A judge with administrative leadership responsibilities for a court or court division, such as assigning judicial officers, supervising calendars, and implementing court policy. The presiding judge is not necessarily the judge assigned to decide a particular case.
Explanation: The presiding judge helps administer the court or division rather than automatically hearing every case.
Example: The presiding judge reassigned cases among departments to balance the family law calendar.

PRESUMED PARENT
Definition: A person who meets a statutory basis for presumed parentage, such as certain marriage related conditions or receiving the child into the home and openly holding the child out as their own. Presumed parentage creates strong legal status but may be weighed against competing presumptions.
Explanation: The law treats the person as a parent because of marriage related facts or a real, open parent child relationship.
Example: The nonbiological caregiver was found to be a presumed parent after raising the child in the caregiver's home for many years.
See also: PATERNITY; PARENTAGE BY HOLDING OUT; THREE PARENT FINDING.

PREVAILING PARTY
Definition: The party who wins a case or succeeds on the main issues; in family law, the prevailing party may be entitled to attorney's fees or costs.
Explanation: The side that wins in court.
Example: The court awarded fees to the prevailing party in the custody dispute.

PRIMA FACIE
Definition: Evidence sufficient to establish a fact unless contradicted; in family law, a prima facie case of neglect may justify court intervention.
Explanation: Proof strong enough to stand unless it is disproved.
Example: The court found a prima facie showing of neglect based on the child's living conditions.

PRIMA FACIE CASE
Definition: A case supported by enough evidence to proceed unless disproved; in family law, it may apply to custody, neglect, or support claims.
Explanation: A case with enough initial evidence to continue.
Example: The mother established a prima facie case for custody modification by showing a change in circumstances.

PRIVILEGE LOG
Definition: A list describing documents or communications withheld from discovery based on attorney client privilege, work product, privacy, or another protection. The log should give enough information to evaluate the claim without revealing the protected content.

Explanation: A party lists withheld items and explains the legal protection instead of silently hiding them.
Example: The court ordered a privilege log identifying the dates, authors, recipients, and claimed privilege for withheld emails.
See also: ATTORNEY CLIENT PRIVILEGE.

PRO PER
Definition: A party who appears and acts without an attorney, also described as self represented or in propria persona.
Explanation: Someone who goes to court without a lawyer and represents themselves.
Example: The father appeared in pro per for the divorce trial.

PRO SE
Definition: A Latin term meaning "for oneself," referring to a party who represents themselves in court without an attorney.
Explanation: A person who represents themselves in court without hiring a lawyer.
Example: The mother chose to proceed pro se in her custody case.

PROCEDURE
Definition: The set of rules that govern how a legal case moves through the court system.
Explanation: The steps and rules courts follow in handling cases.
Example: The attorney followed proper procedure in filing the custody motion.

PROCEEDING
Definition: A step, hearing, or action taken in a case under the authority of the court.
Explanation: Any formal part of a case in court.
Example: The adoption proceeding lasted several months before finalization.

PROCESS
Definition: The official steps for serving legal documents and carrying out a case; also, the summons or writ notifying a party of legal action.
Explanation: The legal steps and notices required to involve someone in a case.
Example: The sheriff served process on the father with the custody

petition.

PROFESSIONAL GOODWILL
Definition: The value of a professional practice that comes from expected continued patronage because of the professional's reputation, relationships, location, or other advantages beyond the tangible assets. Community professional goodwill may be valued and divided even though it cannot be sold separately in every case.
Explanation: A successful practice may have value beyond its equipment and cash because clients are likely to keep returning.
Example: The valuation expert calculated the community goodwill of the dental practice using accepted methods and the practitioner's excess earnings.
See also: BUSINESS VALUATION; PEREIRA METHOD; VAN CAMP METHOD.

PROFFER
Definition: To formally offer testimony, documents, or other evidence for the court's consideration and evidentiary ruling.
Explanation: To formally provide evidence for the judge to review.
Example: The attorney proffered documents proving the father's income.

PROOF
Definition: Evidence sufficient under the applicable burden of proof to establish a fact or persuade the court.
Explanation: Evidence that convinces the judge that something is true.
Example: The mother provided proof of medical expenses to support her reimbursement request.

PROOF OF MAILING
Definition: A sworn statement or certificate showing that a document was mailed to the parties, used to establish service.
Explanation: Written confirmation that a legal document was mailed.
Example: The father filed proof of mailing for the custody motion he served on the mother.

PROOF OF SERVICE (AFFIDAVIT OF SERVICE)
Definition: A signed declaration stating when, where, how, and upon whom legal documents were served in accordance with law.

Explanation: A signed statement that the other side was served correctly.
Example: She filed a proof of service after serving the petition.
See also: AFFIDAVIT OF SERVICE (PROOF OF SERVICE); SERVICE; RETURN OF SERVICE.

PROPERTY
Definition: Anything of value owned by a person, including real estate, personal property, and intangible assets; in family law, property is divided as marital or separate in divorce.
Explanation: What someone owns, like houses, cars, or accounts.
Example: The divorce decree divided the couple's property equally.

PROTECTION ORDER
Definition: A court order intended to protect a person from harassment, abuse, or violence, often by restricting contact; common in domestic violence and custody cases.
Explanation: An order keeping one person away from another for safety.
Example: The mother obtained a protection order against the father after repeated threats.
See also: RESTRAINING ORDER; FULL FAITH AND CREDIT FOR PROTECTIVE ORDERS.

PROVE
Definition: To establish the truth of a fact or claim by presenting sufficient evidence in court.
Explanation: To show with evidence that something is true.
Example: The father had to prove that he had paid child support.

PUNISHABLE
Definition: Describing conduct for which a statute or court may impose a fine, sanction, imprisonment, or other lawful consequence.
Explanation: An act that can be punished by law.
Example: Interference with visitation is punishable by contempt sanctions.

PUNISHMENT
Definition: A penalty or sanction imposed by a court for violating a law, rule, judgment, or court order.

Explanation: The consequence or sanction given by a judge when rules are broken.
Example: The father faced punishment for contempt after failing to pay support.

PURSUANT TO
Definition: A legal phrase meaning "in accordance with" or "as authorized by" a law, rule, or order.
Explanation: A formal way of saying something is done according to a law or order.
Example: The court awarded custody pursuant to state statute.

PUTATIVE SPOUSE / QUASI-COMMUNITY PROPERTY
Definition: A person who had a good faith belief that a void or voidable marriage was valid may be declared a putative spouse. Property acquired during the purported marriage that would have been community property can be treated as quasi-community property and divided by the court.
Explanation: A person who honestly believed in an invalid marriage may receive protections similar to a lawful spouse.
Example: Wife was declared a putative spouse because she reasonably did not know that Husband's earlier marriage had never been dissolved.
See also: QUASI-COMMUNITY PROPERTY.

QUALIFIED DOMESTIC RELATIONS ORDER (QDRO)
Definition: A domestic relations order satisfying federal requirements so a covered retirement plan may divide benefits between an employee and alternate payee.
Explanation: An order that splits retirement money in a divorce.
Example: The judge signed a QDRO dividing the pension benefits.
See also: DOMESTIC RELATIONS ORDER (DRO); SEPARATE INTEREST QDRO; SHARED PAYMENT QDRO; SURVIVOR BENEFIT; DEFINED CONTRIBUTION PLAN.

QUALIFIED EXPERT WITNESS - ICWA
Definition: An expert whose testimony is required before foster care placement or termination of parental rights involving an Indian child. The expert must be qualified to address whether continued custody by the parent or Indian custodian is likely to cause serious emotional or physical damage, and should have tribal and cultural knowledge when appropriate.

Explanation: ICWA requires special expert testimony before an Indian child is removed long term or parental rights are ended.
Example: The tribe's child welfare specialist testified as the qualified expert witness about safety and culturally appropriate services.
See also: INDIAN CHILD WELFARE ACT (ICWA).

QUASH
Definition: To annul, void, or set aside a legal proceeding, order, or document by court decision; in family law, motions to quash may be used to challenge improper service of process or subpoenas.
Explanation: When a judge cancels or rejects a legal paper or order.
Example: The father filed a motion to quash the subpoena for his employment records.

QUASI-COMMUNITY PROPERTY
Definition: Under Family Code §125, quasi-community property is real or personal property, wherever located, acquired by either spouse while domiciled in another state or country that would have been community property if acquired while domiciled in California, including property received in exchange for such property.
Explanation: Property acquired during marriage outside California may be treated and divided like community property in a California dissolution or legal separation.
Example: The court treated the retirement benefits earned during the spouses' years in New York as quasi-community property.
See also: COMMUNITY PROPERTY; PUTATIVE SPOUSE / QUASI-COMMUNITY PROPERTY; SEPARATE PROPERTY.

RATIONALE
Definition: The underlying reasoning or justification for a legal decision; in family law, judges must provide the rationale for custody or support rulings to show how they serve the child's best interests or comply with the law.
Explanation: The legal reasoning behind a judge's decision.
Example: The court's rationale for awarding custody focused on the child's emotional stability.

REASON TO KNOW AN INDIAN CHILD IS INVOLVED
Definition: Facts that trigger the court's and agency's duties under ICWA because there is reason to know the child may be an Indian child.

The required response can include further inquiry, notice, and treating the child as an Indian child until the tribe or court resolves the issue under current law.
Explanation: When reliable information suggests tribal membership or eligibility, the court cannot ignore it and must follow ICWA inquiry rules.
Example: The grandmother's statement that the child was enrolled in a named tribe gave the court reason to know ICWA might apply.
See also: INDIAN CHILD WELFARE ACT (ICWA); TRIBAL INTERVENTION OR TRANSFER - ICWA.

REBUTTAL
Definition: The presentation of evidence or argument intended to counter or disprove the opposing party's claims; in family law, rebuttals may involve challenging custody evaluations or financial disclosures.
Explanation: Evidence or arguments used to answer and disprove the other side's case.
Example: The mother offered a rebuttal to the father's claim that she interfered with visitation.

RECESS
Definition: A temporary break in court proceedings ordered by the judge, usually for rest, scheduling, or review of evidence.
Explanation: A short pause in a hearing or trial.
Example: The judge called a recess during the custody trial to review the documents.

RECORD
Definition: The official collection of all documents, transcripts, evidence, and rulings that make up the history of a case; in family law, the record may be reviewed on appeal.
Explanation: The official file of everything that happens in a case.
Example: The appellate court reviewed the record of the divorce trial.

RECUSAL
Definition: The act of a judge or judicial officer removing themselves from a case due to bias, conflict of interest, or appearance of impropriety.
Explanation: When a judge leaves a case because they cannot be fair.
Example: The judge ordered recusal after realizing he had a prior connection to one of the parties.

RECUSE
Definition: To formally disqualify oneself, or be disqualified, from participating in a case due to bias or conflict; the verb form of recusal.
Explanation: When a judge or official removes themselves from a case.
Example: The magistrate chose to recuse herself from the custody case to avoid an appearance of bias.

REDIRECT EXAMINATION
Definition: The questioning of a witness by the attorney who originally called them, after cross examination, to clarify or repair testimony; in family law, redirect is used to strengthen evidence about parenting or finances.
Explanation: When a lawyer questions their own witness again after cross examination.
Example: On redirect examination, the mother's attorney clarified her testimony about school enrollment.
See also: DIRECT EXAMINATION.

REDUCTION
Definition: A decrease ordered by the court in obligations or penalties, such as lowering support payments due to changed circumstances.
Explanation: When a judge lowers the amount of support or another obligation.
Example: The father requested a reduction in child support after losing his job.

REFERRAL
Definition: The act of directing a case, party, or issue to another authority or professional for services or evaluation; in family law, referrals may be made to mediation, counseling, or child protective services.
Explanation: When the court sends a case or person to another service for help or evaluation.
Example: The judge made a referral to family counseling before deciding custody.

REGARDING
Definition: A legal drafting term indicating that the subject of the document or order relates to a specific matter.
Explanation: A formal way of saying "about."
Example: The decree included provisions regarding child support and

visitation.

REGISTRATION OF OUT OF STATE CUSTODY ORDER
Definition: The UCCJEA process for filing another state's custody order in California so it can be enforced here. Notice is served on affected persons, who generally have 20 days to contest on limited grounds such as lack of jurisdiction, later modification, or lack of required notice.
Explanation: A custody order from another state can be formally filed and enforced in California.
Example: Mother registered the Oregon custody order, and Father did not file a timely challenge to registration.
See also: EXPEDITED ENFORCEMENT - UCCJEA; WARRANT TO TAKE PHYSICAL CUSTODY OF CHILD.

RELEVANT
Definition: Evidence or information that directly relates to and helps prove or disprove an issue before the court; irrelevant evidence is excluded.
Explanation: Information that matters to the issue the court must decide.
Example: The judge found the school records relevant to the custody dispute.
RELIEF
Definition: The remedy or assistance a party requests from the court, such as custody, support, divorce, or protective orders.
Explanation: What someone asks the judge to give them in a case.
Example: The mother sought relief in the form of sole custody and child support.

RELIEF FROM DEFAULT
Definition: Relief from certain defaults, default judgments, dismissals, or orders caused by mistake, inadvertence, surprise, or excusable neglect under Code of Civil Procedure §473(b), subject to statutory deadlines and requirements. Family Code set aside statutes may also apply to specified family law judgments and orders.
Explanation: A party may ask the court to fix a serious result caused by an excusable mistake, but the request must be prompt.
Example: Respondent obtained relief from default after showing that a medical emergency caused an excusable failure to file the response on time.

See also: DEFAULT.

RELINQUISHMENT OF PARENTAL RIGHTS
Definition: A legal process in which a parent voluntarily surrenders their rights and responsibilities to their child, often in preparation for adoption.
Explanation: When a parent gives up their legal rights to their child.
Example: The father completed paperwork for relinquishment of parental rights so the child could be adopted by relatives.
See also: TERMINATION OF PARENTAL RIGHTS; ADOPTION.

RELOCATION
Definition: A proposed change in a child's residence that may substantially affect an existing custody or parenting plan. A parent entitled to custody has a statutory right to change the child's residence subject to the court's power to restrain a move that would prejudice the child's rights or welfare; whether court action is needed depends on the order, notice requirements, and the effect on custody.
Explanation: A parent may have a right to move, but a move that disrupts the parenting plan can lead to notice, mediation, or a custody modification proceeding.
Example: The parent requested a new long distance parenting plan because the proposed move would make the existing schedule impractical.
See also: MOVE AWAY CASE; NOTICE OF RELOCATION; CONDON SAFEGUARDS.

RENDER A VERDICT
Definition: To deliver a formal decision. A jury returns a verdict; a judge ordinarily renders a decision, ruling, order, or judgment. Because California family law trials are generally bench trials, "render a verdict" is usually not the proper phrase for a custody or support decision.
Explanation: Juries return verdicts, while family court judges issue rulings, findings, orders, and judgments.
Example: After the bench trial, the judge issued findings and entered a custody order.

REPRODUCTIVE COERCION
Definition: Control over another person's reproductive choices through force, threats, intimidation, or other coercive tactics. California's current

domestic violence law includes unreasonable pressure to become pregnant, interference with contraception or reproductive information, and coercion concerning pregnancy outcomes.
Explanation: Abuse can include forcing or pressuring someone about pregnancy, birth control, or pregnancy decisions.
Example: The court considered evidence that Husband hid contraception and threatened Wife if she did not become pregnant.
See also: COERCIVE CONTROL.

REQUEST
Definition: A formal application or motion made to the court asking for specific relief or action; in family law, requests often involve changes to custody, visitation, or support.
Explanation: Asking the judge to make a decision or grant something.
Example: The mother filed a request for a change in visitation due to her new work schedule.

REQUEST FOR ADMISSION
Definition: A discovery request asking another party to admit or deny specific facts, the application of law to fact, opinions, or the genuineness of documents. A matter may be deemed admitted if the response is late or legally insufficient and the required procedures are followed.
Explanation: The request asks the other side to agree that certain facts or documents are genuine so trial can focus on real disputes.
Example: Wife asked Husband to admit that the attached bank statement was genuine and that the account existed on the separation date.

REQUEST FOR ORDER (RFO)
Definition: California's standard noticed motion in an existing family law case, commonly filed on form FL-300. An RFO may seek temporary, postjudgment, or other orders concerning custody, support, fees, property, enforcement, or related relief.
Explanation: The RFO is the main form used to ask the family court for an order after the case has started.
Example: Father filed an RFO to modify parenting time and recalculate child support.
See also: RESPONSIVE DECLARATION TO REQUEST FOR ORDER; FINDINGS AND ORDER AFTER HEARING (FOAH).

REQUEST FOR PRODUCTION

Definition: A discovery demand requiring another party to produce documents, electronically stored information, tangible things, or access for inspection. The request must describe the items with reasonable detail, and the response must state whether production will occur or why an objection applies.
Explanation: A party uses this request to obtain records and other items from the opposing party.
Example: Mother requested tax returns, general ledgers, loan applications, and electronic accounting files for the family business.
See also: DISCOVERY.

REQUIRED

Definition: Something that is legally mandated or obligated by law, rule, or court order; failure to comply may result in penalties.
Explanation: Something the law or court says must be done.
Example: Parenting classes were required before the court finalized the divorce.

RESERVATION OF SUPPORT JURISDICTION

Definition: A judgment term keeping the court's power to order, modify, or terminate spousal support later even if no support is ordered now. Without reserved jurisdiction, the court may lose power to award future support, depending on the judgment and law.
Explanation: The court keeps the ability to decide support later instead of closing the issue forever.
Example: The judgment set current support at zero but reserved jurisdiction because Wife was recovering from surgery.
See also: SPOUSAL SUPPORT.

RESPONDENT

Definition: The party who must answer or reply to a petition, complaint, or motion filed in court; in family law, the respondent is typically the spouse or parent opposing the petitioner's claims.
Explanation: The person who responds to a case started by someone else.
Example: The respondent filed an answer denying the allegations in the custody petition.

RESPONSIVE DECLARATION TO REQUEST FOR ORDER
Definition: The principal Judicial Council form, FL-320, used to state a party's response to an FL-300 request for order. It tells the court what orders the responding party agrees with or opposes and gives supporting facts, subject to filing and service deadlines.
Explanation: This is the form used to answer the other side's RFO.
Example: Mother filed an FL-320 opposing the requested move and proposing a different school year schedule.
See also: REQUEST FOR ORDER (RFO).

REST THE CASE
Definition: A phrase used when a party has presented all of its evidence and arguments and formally ends its presentation in a trial.
Explanation: When a lawyer tells the judge they have finished showing all their evidence.
Example: After calling her last witness, the mother's attorney stated, "Your Honor, we rest the case."

RESTRAINING ORDER
Definition: A court order that protects a person from harassment, abuse, or threats by another person.
Explanation: An order stopping someone from contacting or harming another.
Example: The court issued a restraining order in the domestic violence case.
See also: PROTECTION ORDER; NO CONTACT ORDER.

RESTRICTED STOCK UNITS (RSUS)
Definition: A form of employee compensation promising company stock or its cash value after stated vesting conditions are met. In divorce, RSUs may be community, separate, or mixed depending on why they were granted and what services or conditions the vesting period rewards.
Explanation: Unvested company stock awards may be divided based on the work or retention period they were meant to reward.
Example: The court reviewed the grant documents and applied a time formula to the RSUs that rewarded continued work after separation.

RETURN A VERDICT
Definition: The act of a jury, or in some cases a judge, formally delivering their decision on the issues presented in trial. In family law,

this phrase is rarely used because most trials are bench trials, but it may appear in related jury matters.
Explanation: When the jury or judge announces their decision in a case.
Example: The jury returned a verdict confirming the validity of the premarital agreement.

RETURN DATE
Definition: The date set by the court for a party to appear, respond, or comply with an order. In family law, return dates are used for hearings on motions, petitions, or restraining orders.
Explanation: The specific day a person must go to court or respond to a case.
Example: The restraining order was issued with a return date for the hearing two weeks later.

RETURN OF SERVICE
Definition: A sworn statement by the person who served legal papers, confirming when, where, and how service was made; required to prove that the opposing party received notice.
Explanation: A written statement proving someone was given legal papers.
Example: The process server filed a return of service showing the father received the custody petition.
See also: PROOF OF SERVICE (AFFIDAVIT OF SERVICE).

REUNIFICATION COUNSELING
Definition: Therapy or counseling services aimed at rebuilding the relationship between a parent and child after separation, neglect, or abuse.
Explanation: Counseling to help a parent and child rebuild their relationship.
Example: The court ordered reunification counseling for the mother and daughter after years of estrangement.
See also: PIQUI'S LAW.

REUNIFICATION SERVICES
Definition: Court ordered programs designed to help parents correct issues that led to a child's removal, with the goal of safely reunifying the family; services may include counseling, substance abuse treatment, or parenting classes.

Explanation: Services to help parents fix problems so children can return home.
Example: The court ordered reunification services for the mother after finding neglect.

REVIEW
Definition: The court's re-examination of a case, order, or decision, either at a scheduled review hearing or through appellate review.
Explanation: When the court looks again at a decision or order to see if it should change.
Example: The judge scheduled a review of the custody order after six months.

RICHMOND ORDER
Definition: A spousal support order, based on In re Marriage of Richmond, that sets a future termination date but allows the supported spouse to seek an extension before that date by showing good cause. The order is meant to encourage reasonable efforts toward self support while preserving a fair chance to request more time.
Explanation: Support has an end date, but the supported spouse may ask for an extension before the deadline if good cause exists.
Example: The court ordered support to end in four years unless Wife filed a timely motion and showed good cause for an extension.
See also: MORRISON RULE.

RULE
Definition: A legal regulation issued by a court or governing authority, or a procedural guideline controlling how cases are handled.
Explanation: An official requirement that parties must follow in court.
Example: The judge reminded the attorneys to follow the local family court rule on discovery deadlines.

RULE 5.250 CHILD PARTICIPATION
Definition: The California Rule of Court governing whether and how a child participates in a custody proceeding. The court may receive the child's views through testimony, an interview, minor's counsel, a custody professional, or another developmentally appropriate method while protecting the child from harm and pressure.
Explanation: The judge chooses a safe and suitable way to hear the child's views.

Example: Under Rule 5.250, the court received the child's wishes through minor's counsel instead of requiring open court testimony.
See also: MINOR'S COUNSEL.

RULE 8.1115 UNPUBLISHED OPINION RULE
Definition: The California rule that an unpublished Court of Appeal or Superior Court appellate division opinion generally may not be cited or relied on in another case. Narrow exceptions include law of the case, res judicata, collateral estoppel, and certain later review or publication situations.
Explanation: Most unpublished California appellate opinions cannot be used as legal authority in a different case.
Example: The judge declined to consider an unpublished opinion because none of Rule 8.1115's exceptions applied.

RULING
Definition: A judge's official decision on a legal issue presented during a case, such as a motion or objection.
Explanation: The judge's decision on a specific part of the case.
Example: The court's ruling granted temporary custody to the mother.

RUNAWAY
Definition: A minor who leaves home without permission and stays away, often triggering court involvement or child welfare proceedings.
Explanation: A child who runs away from home without consent.
Example: The family court assumed jurisdiction after the teenager was found to be a runaway.

SANCHEZ OBJECTION
Definition: An objection based on People v. Sanchez that an expert is relating case specific hearsay for its truth without independent proof or a hearsay exception. An expert may explain general background knowledge and may rely on proper material, but usually may not act as a channel for unproved case specific statements.
Explanation: An expert cannot simply repeat disputed case facts from other people and make those statements evidence.
Example: The court sustained a Sanchez objection when the evaluator repeated an absent neighbor's detailed accusations as true.

SANCTION
Definition: A penalty or corrective measure imposed by the court for violating a law, rule, or court order; in family law, sanctions may include fines, payment of attorney's fees, or restrictions on evidence.
Explanation: A punishment or consequence for disobeying court rules.
Example: The judge imposed a sanction on the father for failing to disclose financial records.

SANCTIONS FOR DISOBEYING COURT ORDER
Definition: A monetary sanction, under Code of Civil Procedure § 177.5, up to the statutory limit of $1,500, that a judicial officer may impose for violating a lawful court order without good cause or substantial justification. The person must receive notice and an opportunity to be heard.
Explanation: The court may fine someone for disobeying a court order without a good reason.
Example: After repeated violations of a document production order, the court issued notice and imposed a Section 177.5 sanction.
See also: CONTEMPT OF COURT.

SARGON OBJECTION
Definition: A challenge based on Sargon Enterprises, Inc. v. University of Southern California to expert testimony that is speculative, methodologically unreliable, or not logically connected to the data. The trial judge acts as a gatekeeper but does not choose between reasonable competing expert conclusions.
Explanation: An expert opinion must come from reliable methods and facts, not guesswork.
Example: The court excluded the business loss opinion because the expert used unsupported growth assumptions and no reliable comparison data.

SATISFY A JUDGMENT
Definition: To fulfill or pay in full the obligations ordered in a judgment, such as paying child support arrears, spousal support, or property settlements.
Explanation: To complete or pay off what the court ordered.
Example: The father satisfied the judgment by paying all overdue child support.

SCHEDULE
Definition: A court ordered plan or timetable; in family law, schedules are most often used for parenting time, visitation, and payment plans.
Explanation: A timetable set by the court for custody, visitation, or payments.
Example: The parenting schedule gave each parent alternating weekends.

SCHEDULE OF ASSETS AND DEBTS (FL-142)
Definition: A Judicial Council form used in financial disclosure to list property, accounts, retirement benefits, vehicles, businesses, other assets, debts, values, and claimed character. It is served on the other party and is generally not filed publicly with the court.
Explanation: The form gives the other spouse a detailed list of what is owned and owed.
Example: Wife listed the home, pension, vehicles, credit cards, and disputed business interest on her FL-142.
See also: PRELIMINARY DECLARATION OF DISCLOSURE; FINAL DECLARATION OF DISCLOSURE.

SEIZURE OF ASSETS
Definition: The legal taking of property by court order to satisfy a debt or judgment; in family law, seizure of assets may be used to collect unpaid child support or spousal support.
Explanation: When the court takes property to make sure a debt is paid.
Example: The judge ordered seizure of assets from the father's bank account to cover support arrears.

SELF EMPLOYMENT INCOME
Definition: Income from a business, profession, independent contracting, or ownership interest. For support, the court generally starts with gross receipts and subtracts proper business expenses, while adding back personal expenses, excessive deductions, depreciation, or benefits that reduce living costs when the law permits.
Explanation: Business income for support is not always the taxable number shown on the return because personal or unnecessary expenses may be added back.
Example: The court added back the business paid personal vehicle and family travel when calculating the owner's support income.
See also: NET DISPOSABLE INCOME.

SEPARATE INTEREST QDRO

Definition: A QDRO structure that creates a separate retirement interest for the alternate payee, often allowing that person to choose permitted payment options and timing independently of the employee. Availability and terms depend on the plan and federal law.

Explanation: The former spouse receives a separate retirement share instead of waiting for each payment to pass through the employee spouse.

Example: The 401(k) QDRO transferred Wife's awarded share into a separate account in her own name.

See also: QUALIFIED DOMESTIC RELATIONS ORDER (QDRO); DEFINED CONTRIBUTION PLAN.

SEPARATE PROPERTY

Definition: Property owned by one spouse before marriage, or acquired during marriage by gift, inheritance, or personal injury award.

Explanation: Separate property belongs only to one spouse and isn't divided in divorce.

Example: Her grandmother's inheritance was considered separate property.

See also: COMMUNITY PROPERTY; QUASI-COMMUNITY PROPERTY; COMMINGLING; TRANSMUTATION / MACDONALD EXPRESS DECLARATION RULE; DATE OF SEPARATION.

SEPARATION

Definition: The legal or factual ending of cohabitation between spouses or partners, which may be temporary or permanent; in family law, legal separation may involve court orders for custody, support, and property division without dissolving the marriage.

Explanation: When spouses live apart, with or without a court order.

Example: The couple's separation agreement outlined custody and support before filing for divorce.

SERVE

Definition: To formally deliver legal documents to a party, giving them official notice of legal action; in family law, service ensures due process in custody, support, and divorce cases.

Explanation: To officially give someone legal papers about a case.

Example: The father was served with the divorce petition at his workplace.

SERVICE
Definition: The legal act of delivering documents to a party in compliance with court rules; service may be personal, by mail, or by publication.
Explanation: The official process of giving court papers to someone.
Example: Service of the custody petition was completed by certified mail.
See also: PROOF OF SERVICE (AFFIDAVIT OF SERVICE).

SERVICEMEMBERS CIVIL RELIEF ACT (SCRA)
Definition: A federal law protecting qualifying military members in civil cases when service materially affects their ability to participate or meet certain obligations. Protections can include stays, default safeguards, and a reduced interest rate on qualifying pre service debt, but the member must follow the statute's procedures.
Explanation: Military service may justify extra time or other legal protection when it truly interferes with the case.
Example: The deployed parent requested an SCRA stay and provided orders showing that deployment prevented attendance at the custody trial.

SESSION
Definition: A period of time when the court is convened to conduct hearings or trials; in family law, sessions may involve temporary orders, custody disputes, or support hearings.
Explanation: The time when the judge is holding court.
Example: The custody matter was heard during the morning session of family court.

SET OFF
Definition: A legal reduction of one party's obligation by the amount of another obligation owed by the opposing party; in family law, set offs may apply to debts or support arrears.
Explanation: When one debt is reduced because the other side also owes money.
Example: The court applied a set off, reducing the father's arrears by the mother's unpaid share of medical costs.

SETTLE
Definition: To resolve a dispute by agreement without a trial, often recorded in a consent judgment or settlement agreement.
Explanation: To reach an agreement instead of continuing the case in court.
Example: The parents decided to settle their custody dispute through mediation.

SETTLED STATEMENT ON APPEAL
Definition: A summary of the oral proceedings approved by the Trial Court for use on appeal when a reporter's transcript is unavailable or another permitted reason applies. The appellant proposes the statement, the respondent may propose changes, and the trial judge settles the final version.
Explanation: It is an approved written summary of what happened in court when there is no usable court reporter's transcript.
Example: Because no reporter was present, the appellant prepared a proposed settled statement under Rule 8.137.
See also: TRANSCRIPT.

SETTLEMENT
Definition: A formal resolution between parties to a legal dispute, often documented and entered as a court order; in family law, settlements may cover custody, visitation, support, and property division.
Explanation: The written agreement that ends a case without trial.
Example: The divorce settlement divided the couple's assets and established a parenting plan.
See also: MARITAL SETTLEMENT AGREEMENT (MSA).

SETTLEMENT CONFERENCE (FAMILY LAW)
Definition: A meeting where parties, attorneys, and sometimes a judge attempt to settle family law issues before trial.
Explanation: A meeting to try to resolve family law issues before trial.
Example: The property division was resolved during the settlement conference.

SETTLEMENT MOTION
Definition: A motion pursuant to Code of Civil Procedure § 664.6 asking the court to enter judgment under a settlement signed by the parties or stated orally before the court. In a Family Code case, the

parties themselves generally must sign the written settlement; attorney signatures alone do not satisfy this rule.
Explanation: The court can turn a qualifying settlement into a judgment when one side later refuses to complete it.
Example: After Husband refused to sign final judgment papers, Wife moved under Section 664.6 to enforce the settlement both parties had signed.

SHARED PAYMENT QDRO
Definition: A QDRO structure directing a retirement plan to pay the alternate payee a share of each payment made to the employee or retiree. The alternate payee's payment timing and duration may depend on the employee's retirement choices and life, unless survivor protections are included.
Explanation: The former spouse receives part of each pension payment when the employee receives it.
Example: The pension QDRO awarded Husband 40 percent of each monthly benefit paid to Wife and included survivor benefit terms.
See also: QUALIFIED DOMESTIC RELATIONS ORDER (QDRO).

SHOW CAUSE HEARING
Definition: A hearing in which a party must appear before the court and explain why certain relief should not be granted or why they should not be held in contempt.
Explanation: A court hearing where someone must explain their actions to avoid penalties.
Example: The father attended a show cause hearing for failure to pay child support.

SHOW CAUSE ORDER
Definition: A court order requiring a party to appear and explain or justify their conduct or why relief requested by the other party should not be granted.
Explanation: A judge's order telling someone to come to court and explain themselves.
Example: The judge issued a show cause order after repeated violations of the visitation schedule.

SIDEBAR
Definition: A private conversation between the judge and attorneys, held

outside the hearing of the jury or parties, usually about procedural or evidentiary issues.
Explanation: A private discussion at the judge's bench between lawyers and the judge.
Example: The attorneys requested a sidebar to discuss the admissibility of testimony.

SIGNIFICANT
Definition: Important, material, or meaningful in a way that affects the outcome of a case; in family law, significant changes in circumstances may justify modifying custody or support.
Explanation: Something important enough to affect the case.
Example: The court found a significant change in circumstances and modified the custody order.

SIGNIFICANT CONNECTION JURISDICTION - UCCJEA
Definition: A basis for initial custody jurisdiction when no state qualifies as the child's home state, or the home state declines jurisdiction, and the child and at least one parent have a significant connection with the state plus substantial evidence is available there concerning the child's care, protection, training, and relationships.
Explanation: A state may hear the first custody case when there is no controlling home state and the child has strong ties and evidence there.
Example: California exercised significant connection jurisdiction because no home state existed and the child's doctors, school, and extended family were here.
See also: HOME STATE.

SPOUSAL FIDUCIARY DUTY / SECTION 1101 REMEDIES
Definition: The duty of spouses to act with the highest good faith and fair dealing concerning community property and not take unfair advantage of each other. A breach may lead to an accounting, attorney's fees, and an award of 50 percent or, for specified oppressive, fraudulent, or malicious conduct, 100 percent of the affected asset.
Explanation: Spouses must be honest about community property, and serious concealment or misuse can lead to major financial penalties.
Example: The court awarded Wife the full value of a secretly transferred asset after finding fraud that met the statute's higher remedy standard.
See also: HAINES PRESUMPTION.

SPOUSAL SUPPORT
Definition: Financial assistance ordered by the court from one spouse to another after separation or divorce.
Explanation: Spousal support is money one spouse pays the other to help with living expenses after divorce.
Example: The court ordered him to pay spousal support after the divorce.
See also: FAMILY SUPPORT; ALIMONY (SPOUSAL SUPPORT); GAVRON WARNING; VOCATIONAL EVALUATION; RESERVATION OF SUPPORT JURISDICTION.

SPOUSE
Definition: A person who is legally married to another person. Spouses have rights and obligations concerning support, property, fiduciary duties, and, when applicable, parentage and children.
Explanation: A spouse is either person in a legally recognized marriage.
Example: The divorce decree required each spouse to divide community property equally.

STALLWORTH DEFERRED SALE ORDER
Definition: An order delaying sale of the family home and granting temporary exclusive use to one spouse, often the parent living there with the children. Under the deferred sale statutes and In re Marriage of Stallworth, the court considers the children's needs, financial hardship, housing stability, and ability to maintain the property.
Explanation: The home sale is delayed so the children can remain there for a time, if the law's financial and child focused factors support it.
Example: The court delayed sale for two school years so the children could finish at their current school, while assigning mortgage and maintenance duties.

STANDARD OF REVIEW
Definition: The rule an Appellate Court uses to decide how closely it will examine a Trial Court ruling. Common standards include abuse of discretion, substantial evidence, and independent review. The standard often determines how difficult an appeal will be.
Explanation: It tells the appellate court how much deference to give the trial judge's decision.
Example: The custody ruling was reviewed for abuse of discretion, while the meaning of the statute was reviewed independently.

See also: APPEAL.

STATE DISBURSEMENT UNIT (SDU)
Definition: California's centralized system for receiving, processing, recording, and sending many child and spousal support payments, especially payments made through income withholding or cases involving the local child support agency.
Explanation: The SDU is the statewide payment center that keeps a record and forwards support payments.
Example: Father sent the withheld support through the California SDU instead of paying Mother directly.
See also: INCOME WITHHOLDING ORDER; DEPARTMENT OF CHILD SUPPORT SERVICES (DCSS).

STATEMENT
Definition: A written or oral declaration of facts, often made under oath, used as evidence in court proceedings; in family law, statements may include financial disclosures or affidavits.
Explanation: Words written or spoken to explain facts in a case.
Example: The mother submitted a sworn statement about the father's missed support payments.

STATEMENT OF DECISION
Definition: The Trial Court's explanation of the factual and legal basis for its decision on the main disputed issues after a bench trial. A timely and specific request and timely objections can be important for clarifying findings and preserving issues for appeal.
Explanation: The judge explains the key facts and law supporting the trial decision.
Example: After the property trial, Wife timely requested a statement of decision on tracing, valuation, and reimbursement issues.
See also: TAKEN UNDER SUBMISSION; FINAL JUDGMENT.

STATUS
Definition: A person's legal condition or position under the law; in family law, status refers to marital status, parental status, or the status of a child as dependent or emancipated.
Explanation: The legal standing of a person in relation to family matters.
Example: The court changed the parties' status from married to

divorced.

STATUS ONLY JUDGMENT
Definition: A judgment under Family Code §2337 that ends marital status while reserving property, support, fees, or other issues for later. The court may require protective conditions concerning taxes, health insurance, retirement benefits, estate rights, and reimbursement of resulting losses.
Explanation: The parties become legally single before the rest of the divorce issues are finished.
Example: The court granted a status only judgment and reserved the pension and business issues for trial.

STATUTE
Definition: A written law enacted by a legislative body; in family law, statutes regulate marriage, divorce, custody, adoption, and child support.
Explanation: A law passed by the legislature.
Example: The custody order was based on the state statute requiring best interest analysis.

STATUTE OF LIMITATIONS
Definition: The legal time limit within which a case must be filed; in family law, statutes of limitations may apply to paternity actions or enforcement of past support obligations.
Explanation: A deadline for starting a legal action.
Example: The mother's claim for battery was dismissed as outside the statute of limitations.

STATUTORY LAW
Definition: Laws enacted by a legislature, as opposed to case law or common law; in family law, statutory law governs custody, divorce procedures, and support calculations.
Explanation: Written laws created by lawmakers.
Example: Statutory law requires both parents to support their children.

STAY
Definition: A court order temporarily halting a proceeding or enforcement of a judgment; in family law, stays may pause enforcement of support or custody orders pending appeal.
Explanation: A pause or stop of a case or order by the court.

Example: The appellate court issued a stay on the custody order during review.

STEPPARENT ADOPTION

Definition: An adoption in which a spouse or qualifying partner adopts the child of the child's legal parent. The process may require the other parent's consent or a court order dispensing with consent, background checks, an investigation, and the child's consent when the child is old enough under the statute.
Explanation: A stepparent becomes the child's full legal parent through adoption.
Example: The court granted the stepparent adoption after the absent parent's rights were ended and the child gave the required consent.
See also: FREEDOM FROM PARENTAL CUSTODY AND CONTROL; TERMINATION OF PARENTAL RIGHTS.

STIPULATE

Definition: To agree voluntarily to certain facts or terms during litigation, often to simplify issues for trial.
Explanation: When parties agree on something so it does not need to be argued in court.
Example: The parents stipulated to the child's school enrollment before trial.

STIPULATION

Definition: A written or oral agreement between parties that is accepted by the court and becomes binding; in family law, stipulations often resolve issues like custody schedules or support amounts.
Explanation: An agreement made during a case that the judge approves.
Example: The divorce included a stipulation that the father would pay health insurance for the children.

STRIKE

Definition: A court ruling removing improper matter from a pleading, testimony, exhibit, or other portion of the record.
Explanation: When the judge removes something from the case so it cannot be considered.
Example: The court struck the father's testimony after finding it hearsay.
See also: OBJECTION.

SUBMIT
Definition: To formally present a document, motion, evidence, or disputed matter to the court for consideration or decision.
Explanation: To give something officially to the court.
Example: The attorney submitted the parenting plan for approval.

SUBPOENA
Definition: A legal order requiring a person to appear in court or produce documents; failure to comply can result in penalties.
Explanation: A court command to appear or bring documents.
Example: The mother received a subpoena to testify at the custody trial.

SUE
Definition: To commence and pursue a legal action against another person or entity by filing the required pleading.
Explanation: To start a case by filing legal papers against someone.
Example: The wife chose to sue for divorce after years of separation.

SUIT
Definition: A legal case filed in court; in family law, suits include divorce, custody, or support actions.
Explanation: Another word for a legal case.
Example: The mother filed a suit for custody and child support.

SUMMARY JUDGMENT
Definition: A court decision made without a trial when there are no disputed material facts and one party is entitled to judgment as a matter of law.
Explanation: A ruling made by the judge without a trial because the facts are clear.
Example: The father moved for summary judgment in the support enforcement action.

SUMMATION
Definition: The final argument made by attorneys at the close of a trial, summarizing evidence and urging a favorable decision.
Explanation: The lawyer's closing remarks at the end of trial.
Example: In her summation, the mother's attorney stressed the child's need for stability.

SUMMONS
Definition: A formal court notice informing the respondent that a case has been filed and stating the deadline and consequences for filing a response. A summons does not always require the person to appear at a particular hearing.
Explanation: It tells the respondent about the case and how long they have to respond.
Example: The father was served with a summons in the divorce action.

SUPERIOR COURT
Definition: A trial level court of general jurisdiction that hears civil and criminal cases, including family law matters such as divorce, custody, adoption, and support.
Explanation: The main trial court that decides important cases, including family cases.
Example: The custody petition was filed in the superior court.

SUPERVISED VISITATION
Definition: Court ordered parenting time conducted in the presence of an approved monitor to protect a child's safety and welfare.
Explanation: Supervised visitation means a parent can only see the child while another adult is present.
Example: The judge granted supervised visitation due to safety concerns.
See also: VISITATION; COURT ORDERED SUPERVISED VISITATION; VISITATION MONITOR; VISITATION CENTER; BATTERER INTERVENTION PROGRAM (BIP).

SUPPORT RETROACTIVITY
Definition: The rules controlling how far back a child- or spousal support order may begin. An initial child support order may generally reach back to the filing of the initiating paper, subject to service limits. A modification or termination usually may reach back only to the filing date of the modification request or another date allowed by statute.
Explanation: Support usually cannot be changed for months before the proper request was filed.
Example: The court reduced support effective on the date Father filed his modification request, not the earlier date when his income first dropped.
See also: INTEREST ON SUPPORT ARREARS; MOTION TO

MODIFY SUPPORT; JACKSON/TRAINOTTI CREDITS.

SURVIVOR BENEFIT
Definition: A retirement plan benefit paid to a named survivor after the employee or retiree dies. In divorce, a survivor benefit may be needed to protect the former spouse's pension share, and the order should address election, cost, beneficiary status, and what happens after remarriage or death.
Explanation: This benefit can keep pension payments going to a former spouse after the employee spouse dies.
Example: The judgment required Husband to elect a former spouse survivor benefit so Wife's pension share would not end at his death.
See also: QUALIFIED DOMESTIC RELATIONS ORDER (QDRO); MILITARY RETIRED PAY - 10/10 RULE.

SWEAR IN
Definition: The formal act of administering an oath to a witness, juror, or party, requiring them to promise to tell the truth or perform their duties honestly; in family law, witnesses and parties are sworn in before testifying.
Explanation: When someone promises in court to tell the truth before speaking.
Example: The judge asked the clerk to swear in the mother before her testimony in the custody case.

SWORN STATEMENT
Definition: A written or oral statement given under oath or affirmation, verified as truthful and signed before an authorized official; in family law, sworn statements are used for financial disclosures, affidavits, or declarations.
Explanation: A written or spoken declaration made under oath that must be true.
Example: The father submitted a sworn statement about his income in the child support case.
See also: AFFIDAVIT.

TAKE AN OATH
Definition: To make a solemn promise, administered by a court or authorized official, to tell the truth or faithfully perform one's duties; in family law, parties, witnesses, and interpreters often take oaths.

Explanation: To formally promise to tell the truth or do a duty in court.
Example: The custody evaluator took an oath before presenting her findings to the court.

TAKEN UNDER SUBMISSION

Definition: A statement that the court has finished receiving evidence or argument but will issue its decision later. The judge may request more briefing or a proposed order, but the matter is not finally decided until the ruling is made and entered.
Explanation: The hearing is over, and the judge will decide the issue later.
Example: After closing arguments, the judge took the move away request under submission and issued a written ruling the next week.
See also: STATEMENT OF DECISION.

TAX OFFSET

Definition: A government action that intercepts tax refunds and applies them to unpaid debts; in family law, tax offsets are commonly used to collect past due child support.
Explanation: When the government takes money from a tax refund to pay overdue support.
Example: The father's tax refund was taken through a tax offset to pay child support arrears.

TEMPORARY

Definition: Something that is valid for a limited time until a final decision is made; in family law, temporary orders may include custody, visitation, or support arrangements while a case is pending.
Explanation: An order or arrangement that lasts only until the court makes a final ruling.
Example: The court issued a temporary custody order giving the mother primary care until the trial.

TEMPORARY CUSTODY

Definition: A short term custody arrangement ordered while a case is pending, remaining effective until further order or final judgment.
Explanation: Temporary custody is who the child stays with until the court makes a final order.
Example: The mother was given temporary custody until the trial date.

TEMPORARY EMERGENCY JURISDICTION - UCCJEA

Definition: Short term custody power when a child is present in California and has been abandoned or needs emergency protection because the child, a sibling, or a parent is subjected to or threatened with mistreatment or abuse. The court must communicate with any state that has an existing custody case or order.
Explanation: California can make an emergency custody order to protect a child who is here, even when another state normally controls the case.
Example: The court entered a temporary emergency order after the child arrived in California with recent injuries and an immediate safety risk.
See also: UNIFORM CHILD CUSTODY JURISDICTION AND ENFORCEMENT ACT (UCCJEA).

TEMPORARY PROTECTIVE ORDER

Definition: A generic term for a short term protective order pending a fuller hearing. California family law more commonly uses specific terms such as temporary restraining order, domestic violence restraining order, civil harassment restraining order, or emergency protective order, each governed by a different statute and form.
Explanation: The exact name, duration, and procedure depend on the type of protective order requested.
Example: The court issued a temporary domestic violence restraining order and set a hearing on whether a longer order should issue.

TEMPORARY RESTRAINING ORDER

Definition: A short term court order that prohibits certain actions, such as contact, harassment, or removal of a child from the jurisdiction, until a full hearing; often issued in emergencies.
Explanation: A judge's emergency order that temporarily stops someone from doing something.
Example: The judge granted a temporary restraining order preventing the father from removing the child from the state.
See also: DOMESTIC VIOLENCE RESTRAINING ORDER.

TENTATIVE RULING

Definition: A proposed ruling issued before a hearing under a court's local procedures. The ruling may become final unless a party timely requests oral argument or follows another required step. Family courts

differ in whether and how they use tentative rulings.
Explanation: The court announces its likely decision before the hearing, and a party may need to act quickly to request argument.
Example: Counsel followed the local rule and timely requested oral argument on the tentative ruling.

TERMINATE
Definition: To bring a legal relationship, obligation, or proceeding to an end by court order; in family law, termination may apply to parental rights, support obligations, or marriage.
Explanation: To legally end something, such as rights, duties, or a marriage.
Example: The court moved to terminate the father's parental rights due to long term neglect.

TERMINATION OF PARENTAL RIGHTS
Definition: A court process that permanently severs a legal parent child relationship after the required statutory grounds, notice, proof, and best interest findings. The procedure and consequences differ among adoption, juvenile dependency, and other authorized proceedings.
Explanation: A final termination order ends the parent's legal status, but the court may enter it only through a statute that authorizes termination and after required procedures are followed.
Example: After the required notice, evidence, and findings in the dependency case, the juvenile court terminated parental rights and selected adoption as the permanent plan.
See also: STEPPARENT ADOPTION; RELINQUISHMENT OF PARENTAL RIGHTS.

TESTIFY
Definition: To give sworn evidence in court as a witness, party, or expert; in family law, parties may testify about custody, support, domestic violence, or financial matters.
Explanation: To speak under oath in court about what you know.
Example: The mother testified about the father's failure to attend the child's medical appointments.

TESTIMONY
Definition: The evidence given under oath by a witness or party during a trial or hearing; in family law, testimony helps the court decide issues

such as parenting ability or financial status.
Explanation: What a person says in court under oath.
Example: The judge relied on the child's teacher's testimony about school attendance in the custody case.

THREAT
Definition: A declaration or action indicating an intention to cause harm, fear, or injury; in family law, threats may support restraining orders or affect custody decisions.
Explanation: A statement or act showing intent to cause harm or fear.
Example: The mother sought a restraining order after receiving a threat from her former spouse.

THREATEN
Definition: To make a statement or take an action indicating an intent to cause harm, intimidation, or coercion; in family law, threatening behavior may justify protective orders or limit visitation.
Explanation: To say or do something that shows you plan to cause harm or pressure someone.
Example: The father threatened the mother during a visitation exchange, leading to a court ordered no contact provision.

THREE PARENT FINDING
Definition: A finding under Family Code §7612 that recognizing only two legal parents would be detrimental to the child, allowing the court to recognize more than two parents. The court considers the child's existing parental bonds and the harm of removing a stable parent child relationship.
Explanation: A child may have more than two legal parents when limiting parentage to two would harm the child.
Example: The court recognized three parents because the child had long standing, secure parental relationships with all three adults.
See also: COMPETING PARENTAGE PRESUMPTIONS; PRESUMED PARENT.

TRANSCRIPT
Definition: The official written record of everything said during a court proceeding, prepared by a court reporter; in family law, transcripts are used for appeals or review of hearings.
Explanation: The written record of all words spoken in court.

Example: The mother ordered a transcript of the hearing for her appeal.
See also: VERBATIM RECORD; SETTLED STATEMENT ON APPEAL.

TRANSMUTATION / MACDONALD EXPRESS DECLARATION RULE
Definition: A change in property character between community and separate property. For most post 1984 transmutations, California requires a writing with an express declaration by the spouse whose interest is harmed. Under Estate of MacDonald, the writing must clearly state that ownership or character is being changed.
Explanation: Spouses usually cannot change property from separate to community, or the reverse, without clear written words showing that change.
Example: The note saying 'I give you this house as your separate property' satisfied the express declaration requirement, while a vague beneficiary form did not.
See also: SEPARATE PROPERTY; ANTI LUCAS STATUTES - SECTIONS 2581 AND 2640; VALLI TITLE RULE; HAINES PRESUMPTION.

TRIAL
Definition: A formal court proceeding in which evidence and testimony are presented, and a judge (or jury, in rare cases) makes a final decision; in family law, trials decide disputes over custody, support, or property division.
Explanation: A court process where the judge hears evidence and makes a final decision.
Example: The custody trial lasted three days and included testimony from both parents.

TRIAL COURT
Definition: The court of first instance where cases are initially filed, evidence is presented, and rulings are issued; in family law, Trial Courts handle divorce, custody, adoption, and support cases.
Explanation: The court where a case starts and evidence is first heard.
Example: The trial court issued an order granting joint legal custody.

TRIAL JUDGE
Definition: The judge presiding over a trial, responsible for managing

proceedings, ruling on objections, and issuing decisions or verdicts.
Explanation: The judge in charge of the trial who makes rulings and final decisions.
Example: The trial judge considered the best interest factors before awarding custody.

TRIALS
Definition: Plural of trial; multiple formal court proceedings where evidence and testimony are presented and decisions are made.
Explanation: More than one court trial.
Example: The family division handled several custody trials in the same week.

TRIBAL INTERVENTION OR TRANSFER - ICWA
Definition: Rights allowing an Indian child's tribe to intervene in a covered state court proceeding and, in many foster care or parental rights cases, to request transfer to tribal court. Transfer may be denied only under the governing legal standards, and the child's parent or tribe may have separate rights to request or oppose it.
Explanation: The tribe can join the case and may ask that the case be heard in tribal court.
Example: After receiving notice, the tribe intervened and requested transfer of the foster care case to tribal court.
See also: REASON TO KNOW AN INDIAN CHILD IS INVOLVED.

TRUST ACCOUNT
Definition: An account where money is held for the benefit of a child or dependent, managed by a trustee.
Explanation: A trust account is where money is kept safe for someone, usually a child, until later.
Example: The inheritance was placed in a trust account for the minor child.

UIFSA REGISTRATION AND MODIFICATION
Definition: The process under the Uniform Interstate Family Support Act for registering an out of state support order in California for enforcement or, when the strict jurisdictional rules are met, modification. UIFSA limits competing orders and protects the issuing state's continuing, exclusive jurisdiction.
Explanation: An out of state support order can be filed here, but

California may change it only when UIFSA allows.
Example: Mother registered the Texas order for enforcement, but California declined to modify it because Texas still had continuing, exclusive jurisdiction.

UNCONTESTED DIVORCE
Definition: A divorce where both spouses agree on all terms such as custody, support, and property division.
Explanation: Uncontested divorce means both sides agree and don't fight in court.
Example: They filed for an uncontested divorce since they agreed on everything.

UNDER OATH
Definition: A legal status in which a person has sworn or affirmed to tell the truth in testimony, affidavit, or declaration, subject to penalties for perjury if false. In family law, parties and witnesses give testimony under oath in custody, support, and divorce cases.
Explanation: When someone promises in court to tell the truth and can be punished if they lie.
Example: The father testified under oath that he had paid all child support.

UNDERSIGNED
Definition: A term used in legal documents to refer to the person who has signed the document, typically at the bottom; the undersigned affirms or accepts the contents.
Explanation: The person who signed the document.
Example: The undersigned agreed to the custody terms outlined in the settlement.

UNDUE
Definition: Excessive, improper, or unwarranted; in family law, undue may appear in terms like "undue influence," where one party unfairly pressures another into an agreement.
Explanation: Something unfair, unreasonable, or beyond what is proper.
Example: The wife argued that she signed the prenuptial agreement under undue pressure.

UNFIT PARENT
Definition: A nontechnical label sometimes used for a parent whose conduct or condition is proven to create a legally sufficient inability to provide safe and adequate care. California custody decisions should be based on statutory best interest and safety findings; disability, mental illness, poverty, or an unpopular lifestyle does not by itself establish unfitness.
Explanation: The court must rely on evidence of actual harm, risk, or inability to care for the child, not labels or stereotypes.
Example: The court limited custody after specific evidence showed repeated abuse and an ongoing danger to the child, not merely because the parent had a diagnosis.

UNIFORM CHILD CUSTODY JURISDICTION AND ENFORCEMENT ACT (UCCJEA)
Definition: A uniform law governing which state has jurisdiction to make, modify, and enforce child custody determinations.
Explanation: The UCCJEA decides which state's court can handle a custody case.
Example: The UCCJEA applied because the parents lived in different states.
See also: HOME STATE; EXCLUSIVE CONTINUING JURISDICTION - UCCJEA; TEMPORARY EMERGENCY JURISDICTION - UCCJEA; PARENTAL KIDNAPPING PREVENTION ACT (PKPA).

UNIFORM PREMARITAL AGREEMENT ACT / SECTION 1615
Definition: California's framework for deciding whether a premarital agreement is enforceable. The court examines voluntariness, independent counsel or a valid waiver, the seven-day rule, financial disclosure, language and understanding, capacity, fraud, duress, undue influence, and unconscionability under the applicable provisions.
Explanation: A prenup is enforceable only when California's signing, disclosure, counsel, and fairness rules are met.
Example: The court enforced the agreement after finding full financial disclosure, separate attorneys, seven days to review, and no coercion.
See also: PREMARITAL AGREEMENT SEVEN-DAY RULE.

UNJUSTIFIABLE CONDUCT - UCCJEA
Definition: A rule allowing or requiring a court to decline custody jurisdiction when a person seeking to use that jurisdiction engaged in unjustifiable conduct, such as wrongfully taking or hiding the child to create a new forum. Limited exceptions and safety considerations apply.
Explanation: A parent should not gain a custody advantage by wrongfully moving or concealing the child.
Example: California declined jurisdiction after finding that Father secretly removed the child only to create a California custody case.
See also: INCONVENIENT FORUM - UCCJEA.

UNREASONABLE
Definition: Conduct, actions, or demands that exceed what is fair, appropriate, or rational under the law; in family law, an unreasonable position may include denying visitation without cause, requesting excessive support, or refusing cooperation in custody arrangements.
Explanation: When someone acts unfairly or beyond what is sensible in a case.
Example: The court ruled it was unreasonable for the mother to withhold visitation without evidence of danger to the child.

UTILITIES
Definition: Essential services such as electricity, water, gas, and internet that are necessary for maintaining a household; in family law, utilities are considered in calculating child support, spousal support, and household expenses.
Explanation: Household services like power, water, and gas that must be paid each month.
Example: The divorce decree required both parties to share the cost of household utilities until the property was sold.

VACATE ORDER (MOVE OUT ORDER)
Definition: A court order requiring a person, often the restrained party in a domestic violence case, to leave the family residence.
Explanation: Tells one person they must move out of the home, usually for safety.
Example: The court issued a vacate order so the protected party could remain in the home with the children.

VAGUE AND AMBIGUOUS
Definition: An objection that a question is too unclear for the witness to understand and answer fairly. The judge may require the questioner to identify the time, event, person, or meaning more precisely.
Explanation: The question is unclear and could reasonably mean more than one thing.
Example: The court required counsel to clarify what 'the incident' meant before the witness answered.

VALLI TITLE RULE
Definition: A property rule from In re Marriage of Valli that the form of title does not by itself create a valid transmutation between spouses. Even when property is titled in one spouse's name, a change from community to separate property generally must satisfy Family Code §852's express written declaration requirement.
Explanation: Putting an asset in one spouse's name does not always make it separate property; the transmutation writing rule still applies.
Example: A life insurance policy titled only in Wife's name remained community property because no valid written transmutation existed.
See also: ANTI LUCAS STATUTES - SECTIONS 2581 AND 2640; TRANSMUTATION / MACDONALD EXPRESS DECLARATION RULE.

VALUATION DATE
Definition: The date the court uses to determine the value of assets or debts for division.
Explanation: The specific day used to price property or debts for splitting.
Example: The parties agreed to use the date of separation as the valuation date for the business.

VAN CAMP METHOD
Definition: A method used in California family law to divide community and separate property interests in a business when the increase in value is mainly due to the inherent nature of the business or outside factors, rather than community labor. The Van Camp method allocates a reasonable salary for community services, and the remainder of the business growth is treated as separate property. It comes from Van Camp v. Van Camp (1921).
Explanation: A way to divide a business in divorce: the working spouse

is given a fair salary for their efforts during marriage, but most of the growth stays separate if it's due to the business itself.
Example: The court applied the Van Camp method, assigning the wife a reasonable salary for her work and classifying the rest of the business growth as the husband's separate property.
See also: PEREIRA METHOD; PROFESSIONAL GOODWILL.

VENUE
Definition: The proper county or courthouse in which a case should be filed or heard. Venue is distinct from subject matter jurisdiction and from UCCJEA custody jurisdiction; the applicable venue rule depends on the proceeding.
Explanation: Venue identifies the proper location for the case, while jurisdiction determines the court's legal power to decide it.
Example: The dissolution was filed in the county satisfying the statutory residence requirement; the child's six month residence was analyzed separately under the UCCJEA.

VENUE TRANSFER
Definition: A court's decision to move the case to another county or courthouse for proper venue or convenience.
Explanation: Moving the case to a different court location.
Example: The court granted a venue transfer to the county where the child resides.

VERBATIM
Definition: Word for word repetition of spoken or written language; in law, it refers to exact transcription of testimony or proceedings without alteration.
Explanation: An exact record of what was said, with no changes.
Example: The court reporter provided a verbatim transcript of the custody hearing.

VERBATIM RECORD
Definition: The official, word for word record of everything said in court, usually produced by a court reporter; in family law, a verbatim record ensures accuracy for appeals or future proceedings.
Explanation: The official written record showing exactly what was said in court.
Example: The appellate court reviewed the verbatim record of the

divorce trial to evaluate the father's appeal.
See also: TRANSCRIPT.

VERDICT

Definition: The formal decision of a jury on the factual issues submitted to it. A judge in a bench trial ordinarily issues findings, a ruling, an order, or a judgment rather than a verdict. Jury verdicts are uncommon in family law itself but may occur in a related civil action.
Explanation: A verdict is the jury's decision; a family court judge usually issues a ruling or judgment.
Example: The jury returned a verdict in favor of the mother in her claim for intentional infliction of emotional distress.

VERIFICATION

Definition: A written statement signed under penalty of perjury that the facts in a pleading are true.
Explanation: A signed promise that what you filed is true.
Example: She attached a verification to her financial disclosure forms.

VERIFIED PETITION

Definition: A petition accompanied by a signed verification declaring under penalty of perjury that its factual allegations are true.
Explanation: A petition that the filer swears is accurate.
Example: The court required a verified petition for the name change request.

VERSUS

Definition: A legal term, often abbreviated as "v." or "vs.," used in case titles to indicate opposition between parties in a legal proceeding; in family law, it identifies the petitioner and respondent in matters such as divorce, custody, or support.
Explanation: A word showing that one party is bringing a case against another.
Example: The case was titled *Maria Lopez versus Juan Lopez* in the divorce proceedings.

VEXATIOUS LITIGANT

Definition: A person designated by the court who repeatedly files meritless or harassing lawsuits and may need permission to file new actions.

Explanation: Someone who files many baseless cases and needs approval to file more.
Example: He was declared a vexatious litigant after multiple frivolous motions in family court.

VIOLATE
Definition: To break, disobey, or fail to comply with a law, order, or agreement; in family law, violations often involve custody arrangements, support orders, or protective orders.
Explanation: To disobey a court order or legal requirement.
Example: The father was found in contempt for violating the custody exchange order.

VIOLATION
Definition: The act or instance of breaking or disregarding a law, rule, or court order; in family law, violations may include nonpayment of support, denial of visitation, or disobedience of restraining orders.
Explanation: The act of breaking a rule, law, or court order.
Example: The mother reported a violation of the restraining order when the father contacted her by phone.

VIOLATION OF COURT ORDER
Definition: A failure to obey a valid court order, potentially resulting in enforcement, sanctions, contempt, or other remedies.
Explanation: Not obeying what the judge ordered.
Example: Missing exchanges was a violation of the court's visitation order.
See also: CONTEMPT OF COURT.

VISITATION
Definition: Court ordered time between a child and a parent or other authorized person, now often described as parenting time.
Explanation: Court ordered time for a parent to be with the child.
Example: The parenting plan gave the father visitation every other weekend and one midweek evening.
See also: PARENTING TIME; SUPERVISED VISITATION; VISITATION SCHEDULE.

VISITATION CENTER
Definition: A designated facility providing a safe setting for supervised

visits, monitored exchanges, or other court ordered parent child contact.
Explanation: A safe place for supervised visits or child exchanges.
Example: Pickups and drop offs happened at the visitation center to avoid conflict.
See also: SUPERVISED VISITATION.

VISITATION (ELECTRONIC/VIRTUAL)
Definition: Court authorized contact using video, phone, or other electronic means instead of in person time.
Explanation: Visits by video or phone when meeting in person isn't possible.
Example: The order allowed weekly virtual visitation by video call.

VISITATION INTERFERENCE
Definition: Unjustified conduct that prevents, obstructs, or substantially disrupts parenting time required by a valid court order.
Explanation: Blocking the other parent's court ordered time without a good reason.
Example: Repeated last minute cancellations amounted to visitation interference.

VISITATION MODIFICATION
Definition: A request to change the existing visitation terms due to new circumstances or the child's best interests.
Explanation: Asking the court to adjust the current visitation schedule.
Example: After the move, she sought a visitation modification for longer school breaks.

VISITATION MONITOR
Definition: A professional or court approved adult who observes parent child contact and helps enforce safety conditions during supervised visits.
Explanation: A trained person who watches visits to keep the child safe.
Example: The order required a professional visitation monitor for all visits.
See also: SUPERVISED VISITATION.

VISITATION RIGHTS
Definition: The legal right of a parent or relative to spend court approved time with a child.
Explanation: The lawful ability to see the child under set terms.

Example: Grandparents requested visitation rights after the parents separated.
See also: GRANDPARENT VISITATION ORDER.

VISITATION SCHEDULE
Definition: A detailed parenting calendar specifying days, times, exchanges, holidays, vacations, transportation, and other visitation conditions.
Explanation: The written calendar that spells out when visits happen.
Example: The judgment attached a complete visitation schedule.
See also: VISITATION; PARENTING PLAN.

VOCATIONAL EVALUATION
Definition: An expert assessment of a party's education, skills, and earning capacity, often used for spousal support.
Explanation: A review of someone's ability to work and earn.
Example: The court ordered a vocational evaluation to determine her earning capacity.
See also: SPOUSAL SUPPORT; GAVRON WARNING; IMPUTED INCOME (SUPPORT CASES).

VOID MARRIAGE
Definition: A purported marriage that is legally invalid from its inception and ordinarily requires no dissolution to terminate.
Explanation: A marriage the law treats as if it never existed.
Example: A bigamous union is a void marriage and can be challenged at any time.

VOIDABLE MARRIAGE
Definition: A marriage that is valid unless and until annulled by a court on specific grounds.
Explanation: A marriage that counts unless a judge cancels it.
Example: A marriage entered under fraud may be a voidable marriage subject to annulment.

VOLUNTARILY
Definition: An action taken freely, by choice, and without coercion, compulsion, or legal obligation; in family law, acts done voluntarily may include signing settlement agreements, paying support without enforcement, or consenting to custody arrangements.

Explanation: Doing something by choice, not because the court forced you.
Example: The father voluntarily increased his child support payments to help cover medical expenses.

VOLUNTARY ACKNOWLEDGMENT OF PATERNITY
Definition: An older or jurisdiction-specific term for a voluntary parentage document. California currently uses the Voluntary Declaration of Parentage (VDOP), which may establish legal parentage when properly completed, witnessed, and filed; eligibility depends on the family's circumstances.
Explanation: In California, eligible parents use a VDOP to establish parentage without a court judgment.
Example: The eligible parents signed and filed a Voluntary Declaration of Parentage after the child's birth.

VOLUNTARY DECLARATION OF PARENTAGE (VDOP)
Definition: A signed form establishing legal parentage without a court case, often at the hospital or later.
Explanation: A form parents sign to legally name a child's parents.
Example: The parents signed a voluntary declaration of parentage at the hospital to establish legal parentage without filing a court case.
See also: PATERNITY; ACKNOWLEDGMENT OF PARENTAGE – VOLUNTARY.

VOLUNTARY DECLARATION RESCISSION
Definition: The process for canceling a voluntary declaration of parentage by filing the approved rescission form with the Department of Child Support Services within 60 days after the later signature, unless a qualifying custody, visitation, or support order has already been entered in a case involving the person seeking rescission.
Explanation: A signer generally has only 60 days to cancel a voluntary declaration of parentage without a court challenge.
Example: Father filed the rescission form on day 45 and sent the required notice to the other signer.

VOLUNTARY DISMISSAL
Definition: A party's intentional withdrawal of a claim, motion, or entire case before a final adjudication on the merits.
Explanation: Dropping your case or request on your own.

Example: After reaching a settlement, she filed a voluntary dismissal of her motion.

VOLUNTARY RELINQUISHMENT
Definition: A parent's knowing and voluntary surrender of parental rights or custody, commonly used in adoption or dependency proceedings.
Explanation: Choosing to give up parental rights.
Example: The mother signed a voluntary relinquishment so the adoption could proceed.

WAGE ASSIGNMENT (EARNINGS ASSIGNMENT ORDER)
Definition: A court order directing an employer to withhold child support or spousal support from an employee's earnings.
Explanation: Support money is taken directly from wages.
Example: The court issued a wage assignment for child support.
See also: INCOME WITHHOLDING ORDER.

WAGE GARNISHMENT
Definition: A legal process to collect unpaid support by taking part of wages through the employer.
Explanation: Using the employer to take a portion of pay for past due support.
Example: Arrears were recovered by wage garnishment.
See also: EXECUTION AGAINST WAGES.

WAITING PERIOD (COOLING OFF)
Definition: A statutory minimum time, such as six months in California, before a divorce can be finalized.
Explanation: The law requires a set wait before the divorce is final.
Example: They could not finish the divorce until the six month waiting period passed.

WAIVE
Definition: To intentionally give up or relinquish a known legal right, claim, or privilege, either in writing or orally in court; in family law, parties may waive rights such as notice of a hearing or certain claims in a settlement.
Explanation: To choose not to use a legal right.
Example: The mother chose to waive formal service of the divorce

petition.
See also: WAIVER.

WAIVE A RIGHT
Definition: The intentional and voluntary relinquishment of a specific legal right, such as the right to trial, notice, or appeal; in family law, a party may waive a right to certain procedures in order to expedite settlement or judgment.
Explanation: To give up a specific legal right on purpose.
Example: The father agreed to waive his right to a hearing and signed the custody agreement.

WAIVER
Definition: The knowing and voluntary relinquishment of a legal right, claim, privilege, notice, or procedural protection.
Explanation: Choosing to give up a legal right.
Example: He signed a waiver of spousal support in the premarital agreement.
See also: WAIVE; WAIVER OF RIGHTS.

WAIVER OF COURT FEES
Definition: Permission from the court to not pay filing or appearance fees due to financial hardship.
Explanation: The court lets you file without paying because you can't afford it.
Example: Her fee waiver was granted based on low income.

WAIVER OF RIGHTS
Definition: A written or oral declaration in which a person knowingly and voluntarily gives up specific legal rights or protections; in family law, this may include waiving the right to trial, notice, appeal, or certain claims in a settlement agreement.
Explanation: When someone knowingly gives up their legal rights by choice.
Example: The father signed a waiver of rights, agreeing not to contest the adoption.
See also: WAIVER.

WANTON
Definition: Reckless or willful behavior that shows a disregard for the

safety, rights, or well being of others; in family law, wanton conduct may be relevant in findings of abuse, neglect, or harmful behavior toward a child or spouse.
Explanation: Reckless behavior that shows no care for the harm it causes others.
Example: The court found the father's wanton disregard for safety when he left the child unattended for long periods.

WARD OF THE COURT
Definition: A child or other person placed under a court's continuing protection, supervision, or legal control.
Explanation: A child the court takes responsibility for.
Example: After neglect findings, the child was declared a ward of the court.

WARRANT TO TAKE PHYSICAL CUSTODY OF CHILD
Definition: An extraordinary UCCJEA enforcement order directing law enforcement to take physical custody of a child when the child is immediately likely to suffer serious physical harm or be removed from California. The warrant must contain specific findings and protective directions.
Explanation: The court may order immediate recovery of a child when there is an urgent risk of serious harm or flight from the state.
Example: The judge issued a warrant after evidence showed that the parent planned to leave the country that night in violation of the custody order.
See also: REGISTRATION OF OUT OF STATE CUSTODY ORDER.

WATTS CHARGES
Definition: A charge assigned to a spouse in a divorce case for the reasonable value of their exclusive use of a community asset (such as the family home) after separation. It comes from the California case In re Marriage of Watts (1985).
Explanation: A spouse may have to pay for using a shared property (like a house) alone after separation.
Example: The husband was ordered to pay Watts charges for living in the family home by himself after separation.
See also: EPSTEIN CREDITS.

WEEK ON/WEEK OFF SCHEDULE
Definition: A parenting schedule under which the child alternates residences in consecutive one week periods with each parent.
Explanation: Child spends one week with each parent, then switches.
Example: They adopted a week on/week off schedule during the school year.
See also: JOINT PHYSICAL CUSTODY.

WEEKEND/WEEKDAY SCHEDULE
Definition: A parenting schedule assigning specified weekdays and alternating or recurring weekends to each parent under an agreement or court order.
Explanation: Noncustodial parent has certain weekdays and most weekends.
Example: The order set alternating weekends and a midweek overnight.

WELFARE
Definition: A broad and sometimes dated term for public assistance and social service programs, such as cash aid, food assistance, health coverage, and child welfare services. Receipt of public benefits may affect support enforcement or assignment of support rights, but it does not by itself establish parental unfitness or inability to care for a child.
Explanation: Public assistance programs help eligible people meet basic needs; legal consequences depend on the particular program.
Example: Receipt of qualifying cash assistance resulted in assignment of specified child support rights to the government agency under the program rules.

WELFARE AND INSTITUTIONS CODE (WIC)
Definition: The California statutory code governing juvenile dependency, delinquency, public social services, mental health, and related proceedings.
Explanation: California laws for child dependency and juvenile matters.
Example: The dependency petition alleged that the child came within Welfare and Institutions Code §300.

WHEREABOUTS
Definition: The location or place where a person or thing can be found; in family law, courts may require disclosure of a child's or parent's whereabouts to enforce custody and visitation orders.

Explanation: The place where someone is located.
Example: The mother was ordered to disclose the child's whereabouts after moving without notice.

WHEREAS
Definition: A formal legal term used in the introductory clauses of legal documents to explain background facts or reasons for the document; common in contracts, settlement agreements, and court orders.
Explanation: A word used at the beginning of legal documents to introduce reasons or facts.
Example: The settlement agreement began with clauses starting with "Whereas" to explain the background of the divorce.

WILL
Definition: A legal document in which a person declares how their property should be distributed after death and may appoint a guardian for minor children; in family law, wills affect guardianship and inheritance rights.
Explanation: A written legal document that states what happens to property and children's care after someone dies.
Example: The mother's will named her sister as guardian of her minor children.

WILLFUL ACT
Definition: An intentional and deliberate action performed with knowledge and purpose; in family law, a willful act may include failure to pay support, denial of visitation, or acts of domestic violence.
Explanation: Something done on purpose, not by accident.
Example: The judge ruled that the father's refusal to return the child was a willful act of disobedience.

WILLFUL CONTEMPT
Definition: Intentional disobedience of a clear, valid, and known court order, subject to contempt sanctions after required procedural protections.
Explanation: Purposely not following a court order.
Example: Failure to pay ordered support was found to be willful contempt.
See also: CONTEMPT OF COURT.

WILLFULLY
Definition: An act done intentionally, knowingly, and purposely, without mistake or accident; in family law, willful violations of custody, support, or restraining orders may lead to contempt.
Explanation: Doing something on purpose, knowing it breaks the law or a court order.
Example: The father was found in contempt for willfully refusing to pay child support.

WILLING
Definition: Describes a person's readiness, consent, or voluntary choice to act without coercion; in family law, willingness may be considered in custody cases, such as a parent's willingness to facilitate visitation or cooperate in co parenting.
Explanation: Being ready and choosing freely to do something.
Example: The court found that the mother was more willing than the father to support the child's relationship with the other parent.

WITH PREJUDICE
Definition: A legal term indicating that a case has been dismissed permanently and cannot be refiled; in family law, dismissals with prejudice prevent parties from bringing the same custody, support, or divorce claims again.
Explanation: When the court closes a case for good, and it cannot be brought back.
Example: The judge dismissed the father's custody petition with prejudice after finding it legally groundless.

WITHOUT PREJUDICE
Definition: A dismissal, withdrawal, or ruling that does not bar a party from later refiling or renewing the same claim.
Explanation: Closing something now but allowing it to be raised again.
Example: She withdrew the motion without prejudice so she could refile it after completing discovery.

WITNESS
Definition: A person who gives sworn testimony about facts, observations, or expert opinions relevant to a legal proceeding.
Explanation: Someone who tells the court what they saw or know.
Example: The teacher was a key witness at the custody trial.

WORK SEARCH ORDER
Definition: A court order requiring a supported spouse to seek suitable employment, document efforts, and periodically report compliance.
Explanation: Court tells a spouse to look for a job and show proof.
Example: The judge issued a work search order with weekly logs.
See also: GAVRON WARNING; IMPUTED INCOME (SUPPORT CASES).

WORKPLACE VIOLENCE RESTRAINING ORDER (WVRO)
Definition: A civil order protecting workers from violence or threats at a workplace; related to, but distinct from, family DV orders.
Explanation: Court order to protect someone at work from threats or violence.
Example: The employer sought a WVRO after repeated threats at the office.

WRIT
Definition: A formal written order issued by a court directing a person or entity to perform or refrain from performing a specific act; in family law, writs may include writs of habeas corpus (to return a child), writs of mandate (to compel a lower court or agency to act), or writs of execution (to enforce a support judgment).
Explanation: A written court order telling someone to do or stop doing something.
Example: The mother filed a writ of habeas corpus to have the child returned after the father kept the child past the visitation period.

WRIT OF EXECUTION
Definition: A court order authorizing collection on a judgment, such as levying bank accounts for support arrears.
Explanation: Order that lets you collect money awarded by the court.
Example: A writ of execution was issued to collect unpaid spousal support.

WRIT OF HABEAS CORPUS (CHILD CUSTODY)
Definition: A writ used to bring a child before the court to determine the proper custodian.
Explanation: Order to present the child to the court to decide custody.
Example: She filed a habeas petition to recover the child from wrongful retention.

WRIT OF MANDATE (MANDAMUS)
Definition: An appellate remedy asking a higher court to order a lower court or official to perform a required act.
Explanation: Asking a higher court to make a lower court do something it must do.
Example: They sought a writ of mandate to correct the discovery order.

WRIT OF PROHIBITION
Definition: An order from a higher court directing a lower court to stop acting outside its jurisdiction in a family law matter.
Explanation: When a higher court tells a lower court to stop doing something it has no power to do.
Example: The appellate court issued a writ of prohibition stopping the lower court from enforcing an invalid custody order.

WRITTEN STIPULATION
Definition: A signed written agreement between the parties that can be submitted to the court as an order.
Explanation: A written deal both sides sign and give to the judge.
Example: They filed a written stipulation resolving support and holidays.

WRONGFUL REMOVAL/RETENTION
Definition: Keeping or taking a child in violation of custody rights, often raising UCCJEA or Hague issues.
Explanation: Taking or keeping a child against the custody order.
Example: Cross border travel without consent was alleged as wrongful retention.
See also: HAGUE PETITION (INTERNATIONAL ABDUCTION).

X-CHROMOSOME DNA TESTING
Definition: Genetic testing examining X-chromosome markers to evaluate biological relationships in parentage cases involving limited or unavailable reference samples.
Explanation: A type of DNA test to help prove parentage.
Example: Because the alleged father was unavailable, X-chromosome DNA testing was considered.

X-LINKED GENETIC MARKER
Definition: A genetic characteristic on the X-chromosome that can be used as evidence in disputed parentage.

Explanation: A DNA trait on the X-chromosome used as proof in parentage cases.
Example: The expert testified that an X-linked genetic marker supported the claimed relationship.

X-STR ANALYSIS

Definition: Testing of short tandem repeats on the X-chromosome used to resolve certain deficient parentage scenarios.
Explanation: A specialized DNA test on X-chromosome STRs to clarify parentage when other tests fall short.
Example: The lab recommended X-STR analysis due to limited reference samples.

YOUTHFUL OFFENDER

Definition: A minor or young adult treated under special legal provisions recognizing reduced culpability due to age.
Explanation: A young person who breaks the law but is treated more leniently because of age.
Example: The court gave him youthful offender status instead of adult sentencing.

ZERO TOLERANCE POLICY

Definition: A strict policy that imposes predetermined consequences for certain behaviors, often in schools or family supervision contexts.
Explanation: Rules that give automatic punishment for specific actions.
Example: The school's zero tolerance policy applied to drug possession.

ABOUT THE AUTHORS

Victor VeVea

Victor VeVea received his bachelor's degree in mathematics and computer science from California State University, Bakersfield. He became interested in law after being falsely accused and facing a judge who ignored the law and the facts. Mr. VeVea was able to prove his innocence in court despite the judge ordering Mr. VeVea to proceed without an attorney, refusing to allow Mr. VeVea to compel the attendance of witnesses, and even refusing to allow Mr. VeVea to see the evidence being offered against him.

Mr. VeVea received Bachelor of Laws and Juris Doctor degrees from Northwestern California University School of Law before passing the California Bar on the first attempt. He is the author of multiple books, including Handbook for the Accused, Sex Registration Guidebook, Passing Time While Doing Time, and California Criminal Defense Motions in Limine. He has also written multiple articles.

United States District Court Judge Lawrence J. O'Neill described Mr. VeVea as "an extraordinarily bright person, and… an intellectual vigilante." Despite that praise, Mr. VeVea does not practice law. Instead, he devotes his time to volunteer work, scholarly endeavors, helping people who have been falsely accused, assisting self represented litigants with paperwork, and conducting research and investigations for attorneys in difficult cases.

Bakersfield Paralegal

Since its founding in 2001, Bakersfield Paralegal has grown into a trusted legal document services provider throughout California. Headquartered in Bakersfield, the firm specializes in preparing pleadings, motions, and court filings across a broad range of practice areas, including family law, evictions, criminal defense, conservatorships, guardianships, trusts, estate planning, and much more.

Operating under a client centric model, Bakersfield Paralegal serves clients locally and throughout the state. It can meet in person with clients in its immediate service area, while many matters are efficiently handled by phone, video, or email, providing flexibility and convenience for clients across California.

With over two decades of experience, multiple published books on the law, and an impressive array of legal research tools, the company brings substantial institutional knowledge and professionalism. Clients appreciate its thoroughness, responsiveness, and ability to explain complex legal steps clearly.

In a legal environment where the cost and complexity of representation can feel overwhelming, Bakersfield Paralegal offers a structured, affordable alternative for those navigating the court system on their own or seeking peace of mind in document preparation. Its longevity, depth of service offerings, and reputation for dependability make it a pillar in the legal support community.

www.ingramcontent.com/pod-product-compliance
Lightning Source LLC
Chambersburg PA
CBHW071443230926
51846CB00001B/320
* 9 7 8 1 9 5 0 4 1 8 0 6 0 *